MOTHERHOOD IS NOT FOR WIMPS

NO ANSWERS. JUST STORIES.

BY

ELIZABETH SOUTTER SCHWARZER

Bloomington, IN Milton Keynes, UK

authorHOUSE®

Library of Congress Control Number: 2006910499

Schwarzer, Elizabeth Soutter
Motherhood is Not for Wimps
/Elizabeth Soutter Schwarzer
ISBN: 978-1-4259-7643-9
   1.   Motherhood – parenting – humor – essays

About the art: Marc Lutz is the creator of unkymoods.com, a website that featured his unique art and a special script allowing bloggers to choose "moods" for their main pages. They are reprinted here with the artist's help and permission. Marc Lutz continues to make original art at http://unky.vox.com

First Published by AuthorHouse November 30, 2006

Cover design, book layout & design by Carolie DuBose Bartol
Cover photograph by Chris Bartol
Author photograph by Lynne Layman
Interior art by Marc Lutz

Printed in the United States of America

For Franklin
Cute Husband,
My Partner Prince

ACKNOWLEDGEMENTS

This book began as a blog hosted in North Carolina by David Daniels at starfishnet.com. The site was designed and maintained out of Tennessee by Echo Gaines Denmark at creativeechoes.com. This manuscript was edited and both book and cover were designed in Japan by the grammar-obsessed and infinitely patient Carolie Bartol at WordMagix.com. The cover photograph was shot in Tryon, North Carolina by Chris Bartol of Bartol Photography. The interior cartoons were penned by the fabulous Marc Lutz in California. Additional copyediting was completed by Diane Reed, in Colorado Springs, Colorado.

The author lives in Massachusetts.

The lifeblood of this blog is its visitors, who come from all over the world, including the United States, Canada, South Africa, France, the Netherlands, Thailand, Indonesia and a score of others. I am indebted to all of them for their enthusiasm and support, their great humor and their taking the time to send notes and leave comments.

I am grateful to Walter and Lockwood Phillips and *The Carteret County News Times* for being my first regular paying gig, and for being so patient when the deadlines got so hard to meet. I am grateful to Doug Ward for teaching me to write properly, when I thought I already knew. Similar thanks to Alice McDermott and Keith Rupp.

Thanks to pregnancy.org's Mollee, Jules, Missy and Ang for the early support and friendship. To Parenting Magazine and parenting.com for their enthusiasm and support.

I thank my parents, grandmothers, and Emily and Terry for all the have done to keep our contraption of dreams afloat.

I thank Da Posse – Karin and Ellie and their fabulous children. I love you both, and your kids, and it would have been a much darker world without you.

Carolie Bartol deserves another mention here – for she is the reason it happened at all. Thank you for helping me Believe.

And of course my little family: for being the reason I could do it, and the reason it was worth doing.

FOREWORD

Before you begin, I want you to understand just what kind of thing you are reading. The word "barf" appears twenty-eight times in this book. (Synonyms "ralph" "puke" and "hurl" a total of 7.) The word "coffee" appears thirty-two times. "Global socio-economic politics?" Not a once.

I just want you to know what you're getting yourself into. Don't turn to these pages in the hopes of being reassured that motherhood isn't a descent into banality, tedium, and a wider waistline.

It is.

Don't come here hoping to be told you can have it all, and quickly. You can't. (Well, okay, I can't, so why should you be allowed to?)

Most of all, please don't look to me for answers – the kids do that all the time and it gives me the willies.

Our local toy store sells flip books at the check out counter. If you open one to a random page you get a still photograph of Curt Schilling mid-pitch on the Fenway mound. If you start at the beginning and flip the pages rapidly under your thumb, start to finish in succession, you get a little movie of Curt pitching a fast ball straight into the catcher's mitt.

Motherhood is Not for Wimps is just like that. In fact, motherhood is just like that. Any given day you don't think you could be standing more still. But those still days flip past so quickly, and suddenly a year or two are gone.

These essays were originally posted on my blog at www.damomma.com between March, 2004 and May, 2005. They have been minimally edited for consistency.

Together they tell a story of days that crawl and years that fly.

Elizabeth Soutter Schwarzer
Summer, 2006

CONTENTS

Contents (cont'd)

CONTENTS (CONT'D)

CAST OF CHARACTERS

Mary – Tiny little body, whole lot of attitude. Likes cancakes, corn, and doggies who aren't afraid of tummy rubs. Should never be left alone with a Swiffer and a bowl of oatmeal. Heroes are Mary Poppins and the garbage man.

Da Momma – Elizabeth. Formerly a latte-slinging, cell phone-talking Washington political junkie. She still drinks lattes, only now she calls them "Momma's little helpers." (Her "$3.57 Magnum" is a vente latte from Starbucks.) She still talks on her cell phone but now it's to coordinate play dates and pay overdue bills while watching the kid at the park.

Cute Husband – A former Marine, now a law student. It was he who instilled in our daughter a love of getting up early in the morning and getting out to do things. The bastard.

Ducky – Mary's 95 year old great grandmother, namesake, and most treasured play-mate. She prefers to remain anonymous otherwise.

The Beasties – Two cats and a dog. The verdict was out on Mary's arrival. Then she took to the high chair to eat her first solids and after that everyone decided she was all right. She loves to benevolently throw scraps over her shoulder like some medieval princess. The vet says they all need to be on diets, but there's only so many things you can worry about in a day, you know?

Da Posse – Every girl needs her peeps, even hopelessly suburban white ones. Of course with names like "Emma" "Mary" and "Greta;" "hopeless" "suburban" and "white" are kind of redundant, no? Speaking of peeps, Emma's mother, Miss Karin and Greta's mother, Miss Ellie are the only reason I haven't impaled myself on a shrimp fork in the face of living in this pink capris-wearing town.

By the Light of the Moon

Portions previously published in *The Carteret County News-Times*
December 22, 2002

I met my daughter Mary in the beige-laminate corridor of Carteret General Hospital in Morehead City, North Carolina. I was wheeled down there in a bed to see the baby I had delivered two hours earlier – unconscious on the operating table after a brutal labor.

The nursery door opened and a small woman with short brown hair and glasses brought out a very tiny baby, swaddled in the standard issue striped hospital blanket. She placed her in my arms, silky cheek against mine. I kissed her lips, smelling sweet cream and baby musk.

"Hello, Little One," I said, to the perfect little stranger in a pink hat, "Happy birthday."

Prior to Mary, I was indestructible. Life was just life, and the choices I made and failings I had wouldn't mean a thing in a hundred years. But staring at that tiny being in the pink hat was like peering through a high-powered telescope at a fixed point in time: I could really screw this up. A lot. She could blow it with her kids and tell them it was because I blew it with her. And, it logically followed, her kids could blow it with their kids and pin the whole thing back on me.

I saw then that I would never again be as free as I had been, not ever in my whole life, and I hadn't really realized it until that moment.

That was a lot of pressure for late on a Saturday night, plugged into a morphine drip and no place to go.

I lay there frantically reviewing my youth in my mind, wondering whether I had done everything I wanted to do because it suddenly seemed very over. (I say frantic – I was drugged out. It probably took hours.)

It is possible to be at the single most important juncture of your entire life, when you officially are an Adult Responsible for Someone, and feel stupider, smaller, more incompetent than ever before. Nothing quite like jamming a large breast into a tiny mouth in a very dark room when you're both crying to boost the old self-esteem.

I learned not to listen to the perfect people. They're stinking liars.

I discovered that it was possible to make macaroni and cheese one-handed while nursing. Just never could figure out how. The woman who knows caught my attention breastfeeding her son while selecting vegetables in the grocery store. There is no envy like mother-envy, and no limit to the amount of information two lactating women will share, even if they are strangers to each other.

If you leave a trail of cordless phones around your house, it's loads of fun tripping over furniture and diaper pails when they ring. You never find one in time. Even if you could, you can't talk now because the ringing phone has elicited shrieks from your child that would deter even the most stalwart telemarketer. And you've probably stubbed your toe so maybe you're crying, too.

It is so much easier to avert a crying fit than to try to stop one already in progress.

I took Mary out into the neighborhood when she was only a few days old – gearing her up in her stroller with layers of blankets, hat, pacifier, rain cover. I was very proud. About forty minutes into our walk someone pointed out I was wearing two different shoes.

Babies love repetition. I soothed one to sleep chanting "motherhood is not for wimps" and rocking. Endlessly. For hours.

Always use a burp cloth. The viscosity of baby spit-up is unmatched by human engineering. A single unnoticed stripe of it down your back could leave a mark on your couch, and on your hair, your kitchen chair, your car...

It is possible for a baby unfazed by foghorns in a Christmas flotilla to dissolve into hysterics at the sound of her daddy blowing his nose. It is possible for a man with a cold to resist the urge to blow his nose for over two hours.

Routine, schmoutine.

For a condition with no set cause, no definitive symptoms, and no cure, an astonishing number of people feel qualified to diagnose colic. An equally astonishing number of people were oblivious to the wild rage I felt when strangers touched my newborn with unwashed hands.

Those first weeks were raw and startling – who was this woman with the saggy belly and aching body? Who was this tiny trusting baby who alternately screamed until my nerves were raw and snuggled until my heart broke from joy?

Would I ever, ever just get to do what I wanted again? (No.)

Mary's changing table was positioned under a second-story window in our North Carolina home. One morning in the early dawn as I was changing her, her eyes fixed on an especially silvery moon. It was spring, and warm, and a luscious wind was rustling the new green leaves.

I finished her change and zipped up her purple sleeper, stepped into a pair of old clogs, and carried her down the stairs.

The sun was starting to color the sky, but the moon shone as though it were midnight. I raised my daughter up into the darkness and the colors. The baby fuzz on her head lifted with the wind.

She tilted her chin toward the sky, opened her mouth and gave me a gigantic gummy grin.

Oh how dull was the world before there was a Mary.

Child Development Research Project:
The Eating Habits of a Fifteen Month Old

Sunday, March 28, 2004

Day One

5:45 a.m. Subject awakens and demands food. Offered fresh omelet of roasted vegetables and three cheeses. Subject appeared contemplative.

5:56 a.m. Scraping omelet pieces off the windows. Subject appears dissatisfied.

5:57 a.m. Curious "bbamamansdoiamedkaaamamamama!!!" shrieking. I believe she is saying, "Yogurt."

5:58 a.m. Subject smearing yogurt into her hair. Appears contented.

6:15 a.m. Subject in steaming bubble bath. Yogurt-caked jammies in sink.

11:30 a.m. Subject offered macaroni and cheese with broccoli. Appears contemplative.

11:32 a.m. Canine observer consumes copious amounts of pasta and broccoli. Subject again shrieks, "bbamamansdoiamedkaaamamamama!!!"

11:33 a.m. Delivered yogurt with appropriate child safety spoon. Attempts to assist child in eating met with hysterical weeping. Wiped my tears and the subject commenced eating on her own.

11:42 a.m. Subject hosed down at sink. Overalls and onesie soaking in laundry room with jammies.

1:37 p.m. Subject awakens from nap. Offered fruit bar. Was able to reassemble the fragments from the ceiling to achieve a whole bar. Interesting ...

2:17 p.m. "Bbamamansdoiamedkaaamamamama!!!" Subject stripped naked. Floor draped with newspaper. Yogurt delivered at 2:18.

2:45 p.m. Tissue is an effective tool for removing yogurt from nostrils 1/110th" in diameter.

4:07 p.m. Hour spent preparing homemade turkey meatballs with apple, raisins and red pepper sauce.

5:07 p.m.   Canine observer really likes turkey meatballs.

5:09 p.m.   "Bbamamansdoiamedkaaamamamama!!!" Red wine goes well with cold turkey meatballs.

5:17 p.m.   Situation desperate. We are running out of yogurt. Reserves low. Am attempting to thin with apple sauce. Pray God, send help. Am trying to talk to subject, but she appears violent. Canine observer cowering. Shrieking has become terrifying.

5:45 p.m.   New teddy bear sweater soaking with jammies, overalls, and onesie. Found patch of hard crusty yogurt on subject's neck. Gin and tonic goes even better with cold turkey meatballs.

7:00 p.m.   Cooked up some pasta. Threw in the cold turkey meatballs. Made husband eat it. He didn't throw any. Turns out he is capable of not acting like a one year old.

DAY TWO

5:45 a.m.   Subject stripped naked and served heaping bowl of yogurt while sink fills with hot sudsy water. Subject put up quite a fight, but I got the yogurt out of her nostrils.

11:00 a.m. Subject stripped naked and served yogurt. Change of outfit on standby.

2:30 p.m.   Subject stripped naked and served yogurt. Laundry pile threatening to overcome us. Am beating back with a broom. We will prevail.

5:00 p.m.   Subject stripped naked and served yogurt. Have succeeded in closing laundry room door. Will sell the house as-is.

posted by Elizabeth at 12:02 p.m.

THE BEST PART

Sunday, July 11, 2004

I don't have any trouble saying what the best part of motherhood is.

Sure, it's the sweet hugs, the helpless giggles, the puckered lips and closed eyes smooch. The absolute wonderment that ladybugs fly, dogs bark and dump trucks collect the trash.

But the best part is all of these things wrapped into one – the simplicity of joy that infuses regular life. The unbelievable magic of being the one who makes it happen for your kid.

Mary graced my breakfast table this morning resplendent in her striped cotton long johns. Her eyes were impossibly blue, her hair a wild tangle I refer to affectionately as "chicken head."

"Shh, baby," I whispered. My grandmother, sprung from the old people home for the summer, is asleep in the bedroom off the kitchen. Mary calls her "Ducky."

Ducky's 95, spry as a 90 year-old, and she doesn't take any crap off anybody. We like her. We like her so much we named our kid after her. She thinks we're pretty swell, too, which is why she's letting us live in her house while Cute Husband goes to law school. We take care of everything – maintenance and upkeep, bills, utilities – and she doesn't charge us rent. It's only semi-winterized, so that's a challenge, but she needed a tenant and we needed a place to live. So it's a nice arrangement.

I was managing oatmeal at the stove when without warning, Mary lowered herself out of her chair and padded over in her bare feet to Ducky's room, oatmeal spoon in hand. She pushed the door open just far enough to see my grandmother sleeping (mercifully without her hearing aid).

"Hiiiiiiiiiiiiiii Ducky!!!!!" Mary shouted, waving. "Oatmeal!!"

Come and eat oatmeal, Ducky! Sit with me in your jammies, and Momma will bring enough for two (she gives extra raisins if you ask nicely!) and then maybe we can color together or jump into my deck pool!

"Hiiiiiii Ducky!!!"

That's the best part.

BUZZING THE LAW PROM
Wednesday, May 12, 2004

Cute Husband wants me to go to the Law Prom with him. It is a gathering of law students to, well, prom. With alcohol you don't have to hide from your teachers. (Who aren't there anyway because law professors have better things to do on a Saturday night.)

Mare was eating breakfast in her high chair and I took the opportunity for a brutal evaluation of my closet.

The cocktail dress from my rehearsal dinner was the last thing I wore pre-pregnancy – the Marine Corps ball, 2001. It zips! Yay! And the high I get from the oxygen deprivation will help me get through insipid cocktail conversation! That went into the "no" pile.

My aunt Emily – pregnant just a year before I was – sent an array of her not-quite-the-you-you-knew-before clothes. There were some cute beaded tops in there that I thought might go well with the long satin skirt I bought in Italy back when "Italy" and "buy" (and "long" and "satin") were words I had use for.

I inspected a pretty silvery sleeveless number that didn't look too intimidating. I hunted for a zipper but couldn't find one so I inhaled and pulled the thing over my head. There was stretching... and twisting, and an odd pinching sensation... beads were hitting the floor in a little shower of plastic. One arm was through, the other one wasn't. My hair seemed to be caught in something... oh. A zipper.

"Juice! Juice!" my cherub chirped from the kitchen. "Momma? Juice?"

"Coming honey lamb!" I called, only my face was buried against taut chiffon so it sounded like, "Mwumpha monkey moo!"

"Maybe I can get one arm around to unzipper the shirt! Yeah! That's the ticket." One arm crept along my back, pulling fabric toward itself like a thirsty man crawling across the desert toward water. Almost there! Almost there!

"Juice? Momma? Toast?"

"Mwhumphaaaaa! Mwumpha monkey mooo!!"

Somehow or other I wrangled out of it. Apparently Emily's not-quite-her was still less than my not-quite-me. (Just as well. The shirt wasn't really long enough to cover the fact the skirt zipper stopped two inches from the waist.)

After breakfast I threw Mare in the car and we headed to Marshall's.

Five little black dresses and one funky pink halter later I realized my problem: My body is a modern art masterpiece. Everything has moved. Honestly, I think my eyes have been rolling around in all kind of directions for the last eighteen months and no one has said so.

None of the little black dresses had zippers. (I checked.) This meant they were pretty shapeless. On top I looked like the victim of Husband-Threw-the-Dress-in-the-Dryer Syndrome. On the bottom I looked like I was wearing a barrel. Altogether, I looked like Mrs. Butterworth with a boob job.

One halter dress was absolutely gorgeous (it had a zipper!) but my bra just wasn't quite pretty enough to display in public like that and I'm too old to fall for the "it'll stay closed if I don't move too much" theory of fashion. I left the store empty-handed.

Oxygen deprivation, like asymmetrical body parts, is so underrated.

posted by Elizabeth at 12:04 p.m.

HEALTHY SELF-ESTEEM, ROTTING TEETH
Friday, July 09, 2004

From the first minutes in the hospital, we're cajoling our young into some pretty ridiculous scenarios. (The whole breastfeeding thing is nothing but laughable... but please don't say this to a lactating woman. Ever.)

It really is astonishing the things that children need to learn, that we their parents must teach them. Take brushing teeth: you put this stuff on the bristles, and you put them against your teeth, and you scrub. Periodically, you rinse with water.

Do you have any idea how hard this is?

Well, try teaching this skill to a chubbers two-foot high human being who does not speak English.

"Okay, up on the step stool! That's right. Now here's a little toothpaste. Brush it up in there real good, okay? Okay, yeah, that's good, sucking the toothpaste off works, too. Let's maybe have a little more and try brushing this time. See? See Momma? BRUSH your teeth. BRUSH – right, okay, I think that's enough toothpaste for one day, let's rinse."

I handed Mary her little plastic cup of water and said, "Take a sip, but spit it out, okay? Look, like Momma." I performed the task while she watched in wide-eyed solemnity.

"You try. Sip. And spit." She took a mouthful of water and dutifully swirled it around her mouth while I congratulated myself on my superior parenting skills.

"Now spit!" I said. She nodded obligingly, swallowed the mouthful, and made a kissing noise in the general direction of the basin.

D'oh!

"Okay, sweetie, let's try again!" I said. "Mouthful of water, swish, spit."

She took the mouthful, swished, swallowed and kissed the sink.

"Good job, Mary!" she chirped.

Well, at least her self-esteem is in good order. Her teeth will be dropping out of her head, but she'll feel good about it.

Today Mare is feeling a little:

posted by Elizabeth at 11:28 a.m.

Just a Spoonful of Sugar...

Wednesday, July 14, 2004

There were two things I waited to introduce to Mary: sugar and television.

My theory was this: Mary is going to find the stuff eventually. But I don't have to encourage it. I'm not going to be a freako mother who never lets her kid be a kid and eat crap and go to hell with herself in front of the television once in a while. But the less lure it has in her life, the better.

Then, one especially stormy March week, I introduced *Mary Poppins*. "Oh how cute," I thought. "When the little lambs sing 'Mary makes your heart so light!' she thinks they are singing right to her!" Mary wasn't very interested in the rest of the movie; she just wanted to keep watching that part.

This was so very cute.

Once.

Twice, even. Honestly, as the child's mother, I probably found it amusing that whole first week. But into weeks three and four, I was hurting. I tried to distract Mary with the usual toys and the bribe of a long walk in the jogger. No dice. All day long it was wild gesticulations toward the office (where the VCR and therefore Mary Poppins live). "On! On!!"

She started to take an interest in the other musical numbers, so that was good, but it involved a lot of fast forwarding. I cut it down to twice a day – once in the morning, once in the afternoon. We'd fit some actual activities in there – a trip to the playground or library or whatever. But as soon as we were back in the house it was, "On! On!" Then it became, "On! Cheese?" And now Mary spends every evening smearing herself in macaroni and cheese and giggling at the wacky antics of Mary Poppins and all her friends.

I've got *Mary Poppins* coming out my ears. My dreams are littered with dancing lambs and singing cows. Poppins comes to me in her big white frilly hat, wags her finger and says, "Really, don't you think it's time to scrape the old Cheerios off the dining room floor? Well begun is half done, to my way of thinking."

I tried a ban. We went nowhere near the office and I even relented and left PBS on on the downstairs television for a bit. No dice. She threw herself against the baby gate and pointed up the stairs.

"On? Ooooooooooooon?"

"Oh, please Mary! I'll do a whole afternoon of Teletubbies if you don't make me listen to 'Chiminey' ever again. Please??"

Now Mare's not just into the musical numbers – she likes the whole thing. That's all she likes. All the time.

I've noticed some interesting things in this movie. For example, after a "Spoonful of Sugar" Poppins dresses the children in their overcoats, but forgets Michael's hat. They go out the door, and later in the park he has it on.

Did Mary Poppins go back for it? Doubtful. She is, after all, practically perfect in every way. Hardly would suit to have to go back for a hat, you know?

And then, when she's measuring with the tape she turns it horizontal to read it. On the close up, though, the writing is vertical. Silly Poppins.

Do you know that Julie Andrews turned down Mary Poppins because she was pregnant? But they wanted her badly enough that they waited. And she looked that good at the end of it. Damn little tight-waisted soprano singing snit. Whatever, Julie.

Julie was suspended from cables a lot in this movie. Apparently at one point she was left hanging for a while because someone forgot to cut her down. When they finally did, she made a bit of a hard landing and someone asked, "Is she down?" and in her Mary Poppins costume she replied, "She bloody well is!" Isn't that funny?

Gosh it's amazing what you can find on the Web when you are bored to tears and trying not to wish you, too, could laugh your way right up to the ceiling.

Oh, it's a jolly holiday all right. Jolly freaking holiday. Hahahahahahaha.

posted by Elizabeth at 11:31 a.m.

ALL I WANT TO DO IS GO TO THE STORE!
Tuesday, July 27, 2004

Going through her luggage my grandmother discovered she'd forgotten a magnifying glass. No problem, Ducky, I said. I'll just pop out to the store and pick one up for you.

This was a function of anachronistic thinking – old Lizzie could run to the store for Grandma. New Lizzie can't make a move without substantial preplanning and several pounds of gear.

Nothing will ever again be simple.

"Okay, Little Mare, time to go to the store! C'mon, let's –"

"Corn? Corn?"

Mary is a cow. She has five stomachs, I am sure of it.

So far that day she had consumed two large pancakes, beef stew with brown rice, fruit leather, two ears of corn, two bowls of macaroni and cheese and at least six cups of milk. She's only two feet high. Her innards must be complex and cavernous.

"Shoes!" I repeated.

"Corn!"

We had some leftover from last night's dinner. I dug one out, broke it in half and gave her one. The other I crammed in my pocket.

"Shoes, kid. Let's ride."

She was way ahead of me. She was stepping into my battered, dirty, free-with-purchase-of-perfume flip flops.

"Um. Mare Bear. Those don't fit you."

"Shoes. Let's riiiiiide."

"But .."

"EEEEEEEEE!!"

"Okay. Okay. Wear the flip flops. But how about a sweater, it's chilly out."

"EEEEEEEEE!!"

"Sweater."

"NO!"

"WE MUST GET THIS MAGNIFYING GLASS OR DUCKY WILL CEASE TO FIND ANY JOY IN CROSSWORD PUZZLES AND WE WILL HAVE MADE A NINETY-FIVE YEAR OLD LADY CRY!! SHOES! SWEATER! LET'S RIDE!!"

"Okay!" Mary said, putting on sunglasses, opening the door.

Okay, whatever, it's just to Walgreens, the car will be warm, no problem. She really couldn't walk down the front step in them, so I had to pick her up and throw her over my shoulder. She screamed. One flip flop fell. I gathered it, and moved toward the car.

"SHOE!! SHOE!! SHOOOOOOOOOOEE!!" she sobbed. I stopped, reapplied the flip flop, and helped her walk to the car which took longer because she kept stopping to eat corn.

I threw her in the seat and got behind the wheel.

"Momma? Corn? Yucky." From the backseat, a mushed up corn cob was passed up. I took it, pausing a moment to evaluate my daughter.

She was wearing shoes that were ten times the size of her feet. Her sunglasses were cockeyed, her tank top was wildly inappropriate to the weather, and there were bits of corn in her hair.

"Okay, good," I said, starting the engine.

"More? Corn?"

"Right," I tossed her the other half and we were on the road.

We got to Walgreens. As I was lifting the kid out of the car I noticed the flip flops were off and just figured it would be easier this way – I'd carry her, we'd dash in and out, no problem.

Yeah, you know it was about a millisecond before she was scurrying barefoot through Walgreens, dripping corn, and shrieking with laughter at the sheer joy of it all.

I managed to dig up a magnifying glass while patrolling the floor in front of Mary looking out for some horrible thing that might pierce her foot, give her a disease or otherwise illustrate my maternal ineptitude in front of a bunch of very critical strangers.

Mary paused to advise a nice young man that the red Nyquil was better than the green. I dragged her away and then made a devastating tactical error, turning right down the toy aisle.

"BALL! BALL! BAAAAAYBEE!" Mary said, pulling toys off the shelves.

"Time to go, honey. Pick up and put away, pick up and put away." Somewhere in our travels I had picked up a bottle of much-needed detergent, and I was holding it in one hand as I wrestled a Barbie doll from two fat little fists.

So I dragged my screaming kid to the check out line. She was suspended by one arm, slung over the front of me, her shirt nearly off, her dirty little feet swinging and kicking wildly. Bits of corn were everywhere. The detergent was mine only by the barest margin of fingertip.

We paid and left, I threw the kid in the car and tossed the soggy corn cob into the bushes, frantically hoping she would forget about it.

Ha. "Corn? Corn? Coooooooooornnnnnnn!!!"

Oh my God.

Know this: if you ever happen upon a mother pulling out of the store, banging her head against the steering wheel muttering to herself about lost sanity and corn cobs... it's just not as easy as it looks.

posted by Elizabeth at 11:04 a.m.

"MY WORLD WAS CALM, WELL ORDERED, EXEMPLARY! THEN CAME THIS PERSON, WITH CHAOS IN HER WAKE!"

Thursday, July 15, 2004

Last night I dreamt I was called to replace the actor playing George Banks in a local stage production of *Mary Poppins*. I was very nervous because there wasn't going to be any rehearsing – but everyone said it would be okay because I already had the lines memorized.

I was also told that I could speak the songs, ala Rex Harris in *My Fair Lady*, so that made me less nervous about the singing part.

By the end, I'm afraid I was becoming quite a prima dona about the whole thing, lamenting to some cast member that it was hard to be the star of the show when I had never rehearsed with the cast.

The star. Puhlease.

Really, I would rather play Glynnis Johns (the actress who played Mrs. Banks) just 'cause "Glynnis" is such a freaking cool name.

P.S. Not even the deafest of Grandmas can sleep through maracas being banged on their bedroom doors.

posted by Elizabeth at 11:32 a.m.

LESSONS LEARNED

Saturday, July 20, 2004

I can't really remember much of the last couple of days except that it was a learning experience. Here, for your benefit, are the lessons learned:

1) The trickiest part about getting a 95 year old and a 2 year old off together anywhere is the Time Warp Motion Factor. The lady moves at a quarter mile an hour. The kid moves at a mile a minute. Getting kid, lady, hats, canes, diapers, snacks, doll-babies and purses all to one location is a little like trying to herd the ocean.

2) At home, these moving parts are complicated by The Dog, who really must be left out of the equation by putting her on the porch all day. Sure, she's sad, but she's sure to forgive you when you let her sleep on your bed that night.

3) Ain't nothing worse in the dead heat of summer than dog urine on your bed.

4) Local farm stands think corn-addicted toddlers are cute. They're super-helpful providing piles of extra-small ears designed for ease of toddler consumption.

5) Corn-addicted toddlers will share with their pal, The Dog.

6) Dogs who eat corn puke copiously.

7) It turns out that doggie corn puke on the laundry pile in the dead heat of summer runs a close second to the pee-in-the-bed thing.

8) Your offspring's ingenuity, intelligence and cuteness are not foremost in your mind when you discover she has lugged a bottle of maple "brup" out of the fridge, up to your office, and swigged from it in an orgy of sugar.

9) A toddler who consumes a half pint of maple syrup before bed WILL have sleep issues.

10) Which is fine, given the whole pee-in-the-bed thing. Guess we'll all stay up and feed maple syrup to the dog.

posted by Elizabeth at 8:24 p.m.

I'D BE FINE IF IT WEREN'T FOR THESE BATS!
Monday, July 24, 2004

It's an old joke between Cute Husband and me. In any stressful situation:

"Hey, you okay?"

"Yeah, I'd be just fine if it weren't for these bats!" (Frantic wave around head at bats that aren't actually there.)

Okay, well, we think it's funny.

So we're living in this ancient house that is mostly unheated and un-insulated and more than a little creepy at night. But I've gotten used to it, and last night I felt tremendously brave for walking down a dark corridor without hesitating.

EEEK!! (shuffle, shuffle)

Okay. Haha. Old house. Constantly hearing things. Haha. That wasn't really something creepy moving in Cute Husband's gym bag (why do men leave these things in the middle of corridors, anyway??)

EEEK!! (shuffle, shuffle)

Okay. Maybe it's time to turn the light on.

I turned on the light and sure enough that gym bag was moving. I'm not used to seeing that sort of behavior in an accessory. (Although if it were going to be any accessory, it would be Cute Husband's gym bag.) I lifted the edge of the bag and peeked and...

HOLY KARMA BATMAN IT'S A FREAKING BAT!!!

"EEEEEEEEEEEEEEEEEEEEEEEKAAAAAAAAAAAAAAAAAAAAAAAAAAAAHHHH-HHHHHHHHHHHHHHHH!!!!" (That one was me.)

It had little batty wings and little batty fangs and – oh, ick! – little batty claws!

I don't think he's peed on anything, though if he were going to I'd steer him toward the dog bed. I don't quite have the courage to do it myself, so the bat can make himself useful while he's here.

posted by Elizabeth at 12:11 p.m.

SLAPPING A DEAD POET
Sunday, July 25, 2004

Sure. Labor sucked.

And the C-section was no picnic. I could tell you tales of nursing that would make a man grip his chest in horror. But none of these are the worst part of motherhood.

The worst part of motherhood for me has been, from the very beginning, mornings. I make rookie mistakes in the morning that I would never make mid-afternoon.

The worst feeling in the world for me is waking up to a dirty house, which is what happened a few days ago. I needed it clean before I could even begin to do anything else. So after I made Mary's oatmeal, I hooked up the Swiffer - got the little soaky pad on the end and started running it along the floor to pick up dog hair and kid drool and whatever-all else godawful is on that floor. But I got distracted, and went off to do something useful like pick up miniscule pieces of diaper cotton ground into the carpet after the dog's afternoon snack the day before. I left the Swiffer with Mary.

"Help? Momma?" I was so absorbed in what I was doing it took a second to register the meek panic in her voice. I darted into the room and stared at the scene that met me.

It is always difficult to reconstruct events for which we were not present, but based on the evidence, here is what I think happened:

Mary spilled some oatmeal. She picked up the Swiffer and Swiffered it around the hardwood for a bit. That seemed like fun, so she spilled some more oatmeal, Swiffered, more oatmeal, more Swiffer.

Oatmeal + Swiffer cleaner = slick as a politician in November.

Mary was stranded on a four inch patch of un-Swiffermealed floor. Streaks of Swiffered oatmeal along her legs suggested to me that she had tried to walk and slipped around in the stuff.

"UP! UP!" she said tersely.

And that was a good morning. On the days she's up and chipper at five, I just want to die.

I was up late one night last week trying to finish a column. This is a sure-fire way to guarantee an early wakeup the following morning. Sure enough, 5:45 a.m.

found me staggering around, bleary-eyed in pursuit of a small fuzzy-headed being in striped pajamas.

"TEETH!" she shouted, climbing up on the foot stool in front of the sink.

"Right, yeah, teeth," I said, vaguely registering that my offspring was standing precariously on the edge of an object of furniture. That's bad, Lizzie's brain said. Toddler balancing on furniture, BAD!

So, naturally, I moved the stool.

Mary, naturally, was catapulted backward where she hit the wall and slid into a heap on the floor.

"Mare? You okay??" She looked startled. Her face contorted into that look of deep betrayal that could become a sob at any minute. "That's right, honey, walk it off, just walk it off." She climbed back up, brushed her teeth, kissed the sink, and we were on our way.

Downstairs, I felt around in the fog for the coffee pot that was set to go off at seven. I turned it to on and rested my head against the refrigerator.

"CANCAKES?" Mary chirped. No pancakes, honey, brain said. No pancakes.

I smelled coffee. I poured some. Milk, brain said. Must find milk. Milk goes in coffee.

I reached over and opened the fridge, beaning my child and sending her sprawling onto the kitchen floor.

Oh. Shit, brain said. Forgot about her.

"Momma?" Mary whimpered, rubbing her head in wounded shock. You are low, brain said. Low, low, low...

In an effort not to do any more damage, I removed my child to the safety of the office and turned on the tube before I went back to the kitchen to make oatmeal. I came back up the stairs balancing two steaming bowls and my coffee. I was still too tired to say much, but brain was happy to see Mary looking enthused over oatmeal.

Oopsie, brain said. Spilled coffee. Must clean up spilled coffee.

"Hi, Momma! Yay oatm – waaaaaaaaaaaaaaa!"

THUD.

I have a "carpe diem" mug and, truthfully, at six in the morning the words do not make me want to seize the day. They make me want to slap a dead poet. – Joanne Sherman

Today Mare is feeling:

posted by Elizabeth at 11:46 a.m.

WORKING GIRL
Saturday, July 28, 2004

I had a call-in radio interview tonight. I still do them periodically, for fun. After a few years as a press secretary and then a few more as a radio show host, I'm good filler. Better than dead air, anyway.

Most nights.

Mary passed on the macaroni and cheese bribe and elected to sit in my lap during the interview, which is always a mistake.

This is how it went:

"The problem isn't with lawyers, per se. The problem is that personal conscience is dead –"

"Mama Dada CAR."

"– you can only sue so many lawyers and doctors for thinking for themselves, taking risks, before you have a system –"

"MAMA!! MAMA!! DADA CAAAAAAAR!"

"– that doesn't allow for personal judgment so only people without any go very far. That's when you get massive torts and these lawyers who don't have a conscience, just an unbelievable drive for money –"

"MAMA!!! MAMA!!! DADA CAAAAAAAAAR. To WOOOOOOOOORK!!!"

"– yes. Mary. Dada took the car to work."

"Dada. Car. To woooork."

"Thank you so much for sharing that with the Eastern North Carolina seaboard."

"Dada. Car. Woooork."

"Yes, baby. That's just exactly right, honey, well done."

"Elizabeth, your daughter sounds like a charmer."

"Oh. Haha. She is."

"And where does Daddy work?"

"Oh. Um. He's a law student. Actually."

Today Mare is feeling:

posted by Elizabeth at 11:29 a.m.

CONVERSATION WITH A TODDLER

Wednesday, August 04, 2004

"MAMA!"

"Yes?"

"MAMA!"

"Yes?"

"MAMA!"

"Yes?"

"MAMA!"

"Yes?"

"MAMA!"

"Yes?"

(Satisfied.) "Mama."

(Satisfied, too.) "Yes."

posted by Elizabeth at 8:17 a.m.

Moving the Herd
Monday, August 09, 2004

Here's the thing about boiling oil the barbarians never tell you: once it bubbles, it bubbles a lot. It bubbles over.

It was our last night before vacation, and I was making fish and chips. I make badass fish and chips.

So anyway, as the flames were climbing the kitchen wall, I was thinking to myself, "Hmmm... man. That looks really haha like the kitchen is on fire. Haha."

Once I'd spent a few hours scraping baking soda out of stove crevices and wiping soot off walls, I really didn't feel like packing any more. We're going to the Berkshires to my Aunt Emily and Uncle Terry's place. But it was late, and fighting fires is exhausting, so Cute Husband and I decided we'd go ahead and get to bed and just get an early start in the morning.

Don't all bad travel stories start with that idea?

So first thing the next morning I wandered downstairs to see what the Magic Sacred Coffeemaker had brewed for me with the nifty automatic timer thingy that is the Saving Grace of All Mothers. That was when I noticed something distinctly odd. Our front door was open.

Wide open.

A quick check showed nothing missing. Except, notably, the dog, who was last seen passed out on the couch.

So out into the morning I went. About twenty minutes into my hard-target search I came across the Sullivan house. They, too, were having front door issues. Namely, that their screen had a massive hole in it. I looked at that hole and I knew.

"Ginny?? Here, puppy puppy!" I whispered through the hole. Ginny came bounding along, bathrobed Dr. Sullivan just steps behind.

"Oh. Haha. Hi."

"Hello. Nice dog. She crawled into my bed early this morning." (I swear I don't know WHERE she learned that.) "Went ahead and gave her breakfast. A goose sausage."

"Sausage? Oh sure, she'll never want to run away again."

Back at the house, Cute Husband was insistent that one of the cats was missing, too. I didn't quite believe him until I was taking a load of stuff out to the car and saw something fat and slow skitter out from behind a rock and dive under the house.

Just our luck.

I crawled under there on my belly and attempted to get a look at him. Here's the thing though: You can't "get a look" at a black cat under a dark house with no flashlight. What I did "get a look at" was icky stuff that stuck to me and my hair and smelled funny and may even have crawled.

There was a flashlight in Ducky's room when she was with us, but she was always a little confused as to who it belonged to and now I couldn't find it so I figured she took it home. Note to buy a new flashlight.

Short of a flashlight, the only way to locate that cat was to go in after him. And you know I wasn't volunteering for that.

Cute Husband concluded that the best thing to do was to suit up for war ~ so that's exactly what he did. He cracked out the digital desert camo, the boots, the whole deal.

It's hard not to adore a man who'll get into camo for your cat.

"Godspeed," I said, as he proceeded to belly crawl under the house like there was automatic weapons fire overhead. Figuring it would take a while, I went ahead and kept loading the car.

"HHHHHHHHHHHHHHHHHHHHHHHHHHHHSSSSSSSSSSSSSSSSHHH!!!!!!"

Honestly, I don't know how to type that, but imagine a really pissed off cat hissing so loudly you can hear it through a couple of inches of wood.

Then, "RAAAAAAAAAAAAAAAAAAAAAR!!!!" and

"OW SHIT YOU LITTLE –"

"RAAAAAAAAAAAAAARRRRRRRRRRRRR!!!!"

"LIZ GET UNDER HERE."

Oh yeah, right. Sounds like my kind of party in there.

But he was insistent so I took a deep breath and belly crawled into the unknown.

Somewhere around the mid beam I became seriously concerned that my butt was going to cause some bizarre souped up Baby Jessica replay with people digging tunnels up under me to pry me out.

"Wow, this is cozy," I said. "You and me, here, under the porch. With the cat."

"This is so not funny." The cat was stuck to a pant leg. I say stuck. His claws were dug into the pant leg, but what was holding him was the large fist clutching his tail.

"What do you want me to do with him?" I asked. I, after all, was not dressed for combat.

"Take him."

"Umm... yeah. Lemme think about that one."

Through some miracle of cooperation we did manage to drag him out but we were both bloodied and dirtied and in foul moods.

We put the cats in the carrier with a certain degree of glee and headed off to the kennel. Mary insisted on going back to their nice "cat condo" (total rip off – it's a white cage with a little carpeting. It's not like a real condo with a fold out or anything) to say goodbye.

They looked pretty dejected when we left.

And who says family vacation is no fun?

posted by Elizabeth at 11:36 p.m.

A Solemn Vow

Friday, August 13, 2004

When I started this blog I promised myself I would never ever talk about potty things:

1) because it's gross;

2) because motherhood has cost me enough dignity without resorting to that;

3) because there is enough here that Mary's going to be pissed about when she's twelve.

So for all of these reasons I can't tell you about Mary's first experience with enchiladas – nor how utterly hysterical she found their effects on her body, and how it kept her giggling an entire afternoon.

You'll just have to imagine it.

Mary is feeling very:

posted by Elizabeth at 12:11 p.m.

Bowling with Champagne
Monday, August 16, 2004

"Okay, you know what I want to do by the time I am thirty? I want to run a marathon."

We were sitting in a lovely Mexican dive in Lenox, Massachusetts, scarfing down guacamole with cold beer. It was Cute Husband's 29th, the kid was with Aunt Emily and we were totally alone like two real grown ups.

"Yeah. I remember you said that."

"I also want to jump out of a perfectly good airplane," Cute Husband said.

"Okedoke," I said.

"What about you? What do you want to do before you are thirty?"

"Um... I want to eat more fruit. Did you notice how Emily and Terry's kids eat so much fruit?"

"That's dumb."

"It's not dumb! Very few Americans eat enough fruit."

"Pick something better. Like jumping out of an airplane."

"Jumping out of an airplane is a better goal than eating fruit? That's irrational. Fruit is cheaper and safer."

"Fine. You eat more fruit. Before I am thirty I want to gamble at a real casino."

"Before I am thirty I want to learn to handle the finances better."

"I didn't finish. I want to gamble at a real casino... with you on my arm in cowboy boots."

"I actually have cowboy boots."

"NOW you're getting the hang of this."

"Okay. Before I am thirty I want to not buy a new car. Ol' Nattie's hanging in at 200,000 miles and I really think she can go another year, which we need –"

"Waiter? Dos margaritas right damn quick, please! Pick something else. Pick something better."

"Before I am thirty I want –"

"If you say, 'to balance my own checkbook' the night is over."

"You know that being better with money is a major thing for me."

"Sweet merciful –"

"OKAY! Before I am thirty, I want to skinny dip in the ocean."

"HOT DAMN!"

"Your turn."

"Before I am thirty I want to go bowling and drink champagne."

"Eh?"

"There's a place. In town. You bowl and they serve champagne."

"I do think we should drink champagne in rented shoes before we die," I conceded.

We paid for our dinner and wandered outside.

"You do know what it is today?" I said.

"International Franklin Day," my husband responded. "Duh."

"Well, yeah. It's also tax free day in Massachusetts. If you're going to buy art, today is the day to do it." I grabbed his hand and we ducked into a pristine, brightly lit shop where a woman in shiny jewelry was fussing with a tissue paper flower arrangement.

"Darling," I gasped delicately, "look!" On the low shelf was a collection of exquisitely hand painted Italian ceramics.

"For my office?" I said, pointing to a tea set. As my husband hyperventilated, I turned the pot over to read the tag. "Coffee set" it said, "$598."

"It is *my* birthday sweetheart," I whispered. "And you know how I feel about Italian ceramic."

"Er."

"Hellooo!!" the woman sang, breezing over. "Isn't that a fabulous tea set?"

"Fab," I said. "Although by the shape of it... I thought maybe it was a coffee set? I suppose I could be wrong. It just seemed so."

She turned the pot over, read the tag and blushed delicately. "So it is. I should have known."

"Well, people hardly know these things any more," I said generously.

"Tell you what, honey," Cute Husband said, "I'll keep this in mind for you, okay? Shall we get on the move?"

"Well, all right. But don't forget it's the coffee set I like. I don't really drink tea in the afternoon."

"Okay. Right. Let's ride."

"You know," I said when we were outside. "You really should get me something for your birthday."

"Of course. I'm really sorry I forgot."

"Hmmm... What's in here?" I dragged him into the Lenox Silver and Leather shop and within minutes had him wearing a pink suede cowboy hat and carrying a polished wood cane with – I kid you not – brake lights that flashed when he stopped.

"You look ghetto fabulous."

"I really do."

I examined a cabinet of half-off silver earrings and tried on about six pairs while Cute Husband chatted with the saleslady about her experiences in Alaska during one of her summers as an undergraduate at Colgate.

We settled on a pretty pair of silver dangles that cost $17 even, no tax.

"Happy birthday!" I said as he paid. He laughed.

We wandered back toward the car in the darkness, holding hands. Not quite ready to give up our night, we sat on a park bench overlooking the battered Pathfinder that had gone all those miles with me in only six years.

"Man I hope she holds," I said. "We really can't afford a car this year. We can't afford gas."

"It won't always be like this."

"I'm so tired of working so hard and not having anything."

"It's going to pay off."

"Really? Do you think that most of the really successful people... do you think they thought it would never happen for them? Do you think they ever sat on a bench just like this and thought they would never make it?"

"YES. YES YES YES."

"You're good at this. It should be International Franklin Day. You should get, like, a present or something."

"Don't know why I didn't think of it."

"Let's go get our kid."

"You think she's asleep?"

"Either that or she's terrorizing Emily and demanding cancakes... Maybe we should go get drinks or something."

"We're all done, kid. You're wearing the drinks in your ears."

"They'll last longer. Hey. Before you turn forty, I'll wear these earrings again, and we'll go to a fancy dinner and stay in a hotel and try to find a quiet bench somewhere to admire our Porsche from."

"Only if we can go bowling and drink champagne."

"You're on."

posted by Elizabeth at 10:48 p.m.

WARNING: STUNT PERFORMED BY IDIOT AMATEUR ON OPEN HIGHWAY

Sunday, August 15, 2004

posted by Elizabeth at 10:12 p.m.

BITTER ZOO PEOPLE
Friday, August 27, 2004

Once you're a parent, the pressure to Do Things on the weekend is indescribable.

When you're newlyweds, the pressure is to say you did something so people don't snicker and look at you knowingly when you say you just hung around the house.

But once you have kids, Doing Something is like growth charts – you compare stats with other mothers to see whose kid has the better life and most devoted parents.

This is what we talk about at Gym Dandy – who's walking, who's talking, and who has schlepped their children into the city for the arts festival and puppet show while everyone else lounged around the house looking for motivation.

Thankfully, Cute Husband is all over Doing Things. He's got plans. He's got a map, and a motto. "Mary, we strike hard, we strike fast!" he says, to a round of excited giggles. I stravage* along behind them, beckoning a cabana boy who doesn't exist to bring a latte that never comes.

That morning, Cute Husband decided we should go to the zoo. Despite the mild cold soaking drizzle.

He swung by Starbucks on the way to shut me up.

The first attraction at the zoo as far as Mary was concerned was the charming assortment of wet picnic tables next to the snack stand (that was closed because most people don't go to the zoo in the rain).

Under one of the tables was a sleeping duck who, by the size of him, has spent the last several years living fat and happy on dropped French fries. He opened an eye, saw that Mary didn't have any fries, and went back to sleep. So bitter is the life of a zoo duck when it's raining.

From there we went on to look at the snow leopards. A sign in front of the cage read something to the effect of: "CAREFUL! Snow leopards are sneaky! They camouflage themselves so you have to look closely to see them. But we swear they're there."

Well, we're no suckers. We stood there in the rain, looking. Other people came and went, but we stayed. We had paid to see snow leopards.

"There're no snow leopards," Cute Husband finally said. "It's a farce!" His voice was rising in agitation. "They make thousands luring people to stand in the rain looking for animals that aren't there."

A passing family gave us very strange looks.

We did finally move on, and we did see some animals – just sort of moist and grumpy ones. Only the sea otters looked really happy.

We caught up with The Family That Looked at Us Funny in front of a display of coyotes in their natural habitat.

"The coyotes are on the ridge," the father said pointing. Very specifically. "Up there."

"Thanks."

"No problem," he said smugly. "Just didn't want you to be zoo cynics."

Excuse me, I prefer "bitter zoo people."

At least this will sound good at Gym Dandy on Monday. I'll tell them GO TO THE ZOO! The snow leopards were the best, and to wait them out, 'cause it's really, really worth it. Boost the ol' SAT score a couple of points, at least.

posted by Elizabeth at 8:35 p.m.

* I want you to know that three people have edited this essay and all have objected to the word "stravage." Let me clarify here, for once and for all, that it is a real word. I don't know this because I am a vocabulary goddess (but let's be very clear, I so am). I know this because Mary Poppins uses it and I have seen that freaking movie a gazillion-million times. BUT. Recognizing that it isn't exactly in common use, please feel free, as you read, to mentally substitute "straggle," "shuffle" or "dawdle." Now back to our regularly-scheduled programming.

Why You Little...!

Monday, August 30, 2004

Some time over the last couple of weeks, Mary stopped sitting in high chairs.

I could see her point. The high chair is hard to climb into, and not safe to climb out of, so she feels trapped. (Which, I'm not lying, was its major asset from my perspective.) It's fair that she wants the same freedom the rest of us have. Unfortunately, the chairs at our dining table have two major problems: 1) short; 2) hard to clean.

In Lenox, Mare had a chance to try out her cousin Matthew's gorgeous red Cosco stepstool chair. She fell in love, we e-bayed, and two weeks later a yellow version arrived in the mail.

This morning, Mary had her first breakfast – peanut butter toast – in the new Cosco chair.

I came out of the kitchen and found her caked in peanut butter. She looked like a mud wrestler in a Pamper.

I was so angry I had to stand there for a minute collecting myself, trying to figure out what to say.

With a very knowing look of disgust, Mary leveled serious blue eyes on me and said, "Need a bath, little girl."

I couldn't help it. I laughed. But just so she would know what she did was very wrong she only got half the normal amount of bubbles.

posted by Elizabeth at 11:53 a.m.

HADDOCK LOVE

Tuesday, August 31, 2004

Now that she's a little person instead of a cute, insatiably hungry blob, I am amused by the connections Mary is making... and the ones she isn't.

From Mary's perspective, every day is filled with fun surprises. When she waves good-bye to the car, for all she knows the car is going to wave back. It would not startle her in the least if it did. When Mary plays with her Cheerios in the morning, she doesn't know whether or not they're going to look at her and sing "Wheels on the Bus." She would laugh and giggle if they did, but it wouldn't strike her as particularly remarkable.

Imagine living in such a world. She's open to anything.

Right up until she gets an idea in her head. Then she's not open to much at all.

I took her on a quick trip to the market for dinner supplies. We were running way late so I grabbed a nice piece of haddock and some veggies and we jetted over to the zippy aisle to check out. Mary held the bag with the haddock in it all the way out to the car. She continued to hold on to it through the car seat procedure and right along through the drive home.

When we got there, more car seat procedure, and I asked Mary, "Are you going to carry that bag for Momma?"

"No."

"Oh. You want Momma to carry it?"

"NO! Mayme's bag!"

"Oh. So you're going to carry it, but not for Momma? You're carrying it because it's Mary's?"

"Yes." Duh, Mother. Sheesh.

Right.

It took her several long minutes to walk from the car to the door with that bag of haddock. But she wasn't letting go for love or money.

In the house I started chopping and throwing stuff in the pan. I really needed that haddock.

I fixed Mary a plate of veggies and cheese and set it out for her with a cup of milk. She abandoned the fish and made for the chair, pausing halfway up and coming back down. She trotted back to the kitchen.

"Mayme's bag," she said, picking up the haddock and marching back over to her chair. So help me, she climbed with it.

"Mary, that bag's gonna give us a major case of dysentery if it doesn't see a fridge soon."

"NO." She said with a giant chomp of carrot.

Oh dear. My child is in love with a haddock.

Finally, as we were getting ready for bed, it was time for her to unhand the fish. I helped her to say goodbye, and there were tears.

I'm only glad she doesn't know that I pan fried it in a nice teriyaki glaze. Love is brutal.

Mary is feeling:

BROKEN HEARTED

posted by Elizabeth at 7:50 p.m.

Okay! Bahbie?? Oooos?

Thursday, August 19, 2004

The emergence of language radically changes your relationship with your child. No longer are you speculating as to your baby's angelic thoughts; you are being regaled on an hourly basis on the minutia of a toddler's daily experience.

There is nothing quite like the feeling of having your child gaze up at you with eyes full of hope and trust, and say:

"Camanakewick?"

"Honey? What?"

"Camanakewick!" she repeats urgently. "Camanakewick!!"

"I'm so sorry sweetheart. I just don't understand. Can you show me?"

"Camanakewiiiiiiiiick!" she wails, dissolving into despairing tears.

When she does manage to communicate an idea, so great is her joy that it bears repeating.

Constantly.

"Dada took cah woook."

"Right, baby. Daddy took the car to work."

"Mama! Dada took cah woook."

"That's right! How did you get to be so smart?"

"Mama! Dada took..."

Aaaaaaargh!!!

Some phrases she repeats simply because she likes the sound of them - their meaning is almost completely lost on her. Much to my relief, it's lost on pretty much everyone else too.

"Mama nina hut."

"Ahaha ... here have a cookie ... shh ... don't talk with your mouth full."

(If you don't get it, I'm not enlightening you.)

Through Mary's emerging use of language I have proof that selective memory is innate in the human beast. Mary hears the word "cake" once, with the item in her mouth, and can forever recall the word in response to the question of what she would like for a snack. "Please" on the other hand...

"Momma mana me oooooooooos?!"

"You'd like some peanut butter and toast? Could you say please?"

"Okay!"

"Please say 'please' Mary."

"Okay!"

"'Momma may I please have peanut butter toast?'"

"Okay!!" she grins, taking my hand and leading me to the kitchen.

What are you going to do?

Then last night after the kid was in bed, Cute Husband and I settled down to watch the third season of Curb Your Enthusiasm. We were quiet. Honestly we were. But when Larry David cut the hair off the Judy Doll belonging to Rita Wilson's daughter, we maybe guffawed a little.

Mary woke up.

I brought her in and rocked her in my lap, figuring she'd pass out and we could keep going.

But then poor Larry was confronted with the irate mother of a child who just figured out that dolls' hair doesn't grow back and we just couldn't keep quiet.

Mary struggled to sit up, a vision in spiky hair, fuzzy jammies, and sleep-dazed eyes.

"Bahbie?" she squinted, as Larry held the poor hairless doll in his arms.

"No, honey, that's Judy. Sleepy time Mary. Snuggle into Momma's arm, okay?"

"Bahbie! BAHBIE!" she said, struggling to loosen herself from my grasp and sit fully up. No, it totally is Barbie, Mom!

Clearly, in my daughter's mind, her parents had betrayed her by putting her to bed so they could watch the story of Barbie's young life and cosmetic mishaps.

"Bahbie," Mary declared, arranging herself next to us, fighting a slight yawn as she fixed her attention on the screen.

Well, you know what we did.

We totally passed her the popcorn.

posted by Elizabeth at 4:40 p.m.

A Rousing Game of "Cat...Momma. Cat...Momma."

Monday, August 23, 2004

My bed is more crowded than a Woodstock sleeping bag.

The problem with co-sleeping toddlers is that they are way too chatty in the morning.

"Dental, cat, dental!" Mary said, whacking poor Pedro who'd been asleep near my head.

"Gentle, Mary, gentle," I muttered mindlessly into the pillow.

"Cat... hose!" she said. A second later I saw stars when a tiny index finger was crammed up my nostril. "Momma hose!"

"Ow."

"Cat eye!" she said.

I was too sleepy to wince, but I could feel her coming at me. She lifted one lid and peered curiously in.

"Momma eye!" she said happily.

I caught a glimpse of the cat, tail swishing in quiet irritation, looking extremely satisfied at the treatment I was receiving.

"Cat, tummy!" A solid whack to his midsection, followed by a curious lifting of blanket and pajama shirt and a loud, "PFFFFFFFFT!!!!!!" above my belly button.

"Aaaaack!!!"

"Momma!" Mary said, sitting back in gleeful surprise. (You're up!) "Cup? Milk?" she suggested.

"Mary... where's Daddy's nose?" I asked, flipping over and pulling the blankets over my head.

As she crawled toward him I heard a muffled muttering that sounded just like "You are a bitch from Hell" but I can't be sure.

posted by Elizabeth at 11:30 a.m.

EEEEEEEK!

Mary has learned to screech.

I am dutifully ignoring. This is difficult.

"EEEEEEEK!!"

No reaction.

"EEEEEKK!!"

Nothing.

"AAAAAAAAAAAAAAEEEEEK!!!!!!" Sweet merciful –

"Mary. Would you like 'help, please?'"

Pause. Blink.

"OKAAAAAAYEEEEK!!"

###

MEALTIME: PART II

My philosophy is that if Mary isn't offered sugary foods then she won't want them and she can always eat whatever she wants. She's almost two; and it's worked great.

So after a hard day playing she sat in her chair and I dutifully brought her a nice steaming bowl of Annie Mac with a side of raw green beans and apples. I went back out to the kitchen to clean up and was startled to turn around and find Mary standing behind me, holding the bowl shaking her head, eyes wide.

"No?" I said. "Really? You don't want mac and cheese? Huh. Okay. What would you like, Honey Lamb?"

"Cookies."

"I'm sorry – I... couldn't have possibly heard you correctly. I... You didn't... I mean you're my child. Everyone knows my child doesn't say such things."

"Cookies."

"Where did you hear that word?? You mean... 'fruit leather?' All natural, all fruit, sugarless fruit leather! Right?"

"Cookies."

And then the fatal word that made all the pieces fall together.

"*Ducky* cookies!"

D'oh!!

Today Mary is feeling:

posted by Elizabeth at 11:34 a.m.

VAL AND THE CLOSET UNDER THE EAVE
Saturday, September 4, 2004

"Hey, Liz, what's going on? It's Val."

"Hey, Val!"

"Don't you have a cell phone any more?"

"Oh, um, I do... I think I do. I meant to call you on our walk yesterday afternoon but I just can't find the cell. Maybe it's time to cancel the service and admit it's lost." It wasn't until I said it out loud that it occurred to me it might really be time to do just that.

"Don't be silly. Ask Mary."

"Yeah, right."

"No. Really. Ask Mary. She's the one who took it."

"You say that like you don't live three hundred miles away."

"Trust Auntie. Mary has the phone."

While we talked I wandered over to Mary's favorite closet, a tiny cupboard built into the eave of the second floor office.

There, laid out neatly on a little shelf, were two old sippies, a book, my beaded bracelet and Spot the Dog. Oh, and my cell phone.

There were five missed calls. All from Valerie. It's nice to have friends.

posted by Elizabeth at 1:05 p.m.

BUSTED!
Tuesday, September 7, 2004

No one can bust you quite the way your kid can.

"Momma?"

"Mwaumph?" I said into the pillow.

"Go? Do things? Car named Nattie?"

"Sure, honey, let's go do things in the car named Nattie. I'm all over that. How about you make a pot of coffee and I'll lie here making a plan, okay?"

"Okay. Bye bye." She spun on her heel, a suspicious tinkling noise tracing her.

"Mary. Could you come back here please? What are you holding?"

"Keys. Car named Nattie."

"Ooooh... right. Can I have those please?"

"Um. No."

"Those are Momma's keys, baby."

"Car named Nattie! Go! Do things." Long thoughtful pause, as we sized each other up. "Momma. Go get coffee?"

Very long pause indeed.

"Mary. Are you bribing me? With a Starbucks run?"

"Okay!"

Really, the first step to recovery is admitting you have a problem. Thank God I don't have one because then I'd be expected to recover.

posted by Elizabeth at 1:07 p.m.

PASTRY LOVE

Tuesday, September 7, 2004

Mary's world is completely without taboo ~ and she occupies it armed with the logic skills of a drunken ambidextrous monkey in a video arcade.

The haddock has been forgotten. It has been replaced by The Danish.

It is luscious, it is raspberry filled, and it comes in a cool blue and white box.

Mary found Mr. Danish on a recent tear through the grocery store. She put it in her little cart and drove it around for a bit, chit chatting about the latest doggies in the neighborhood. I finally reached in to take it, but Mary yanked it from my grasp and took off in the direction of the produce aisle with that box crushed between two fat fists.

I'm all about gentle distraction and all that good stuff, but she was about to maul that pastry past my ability to discreetly hide it under something, pretend it wasn't mine and walk away.

So I picked up screaming child, carried her back to the Entenmanns's shelf, and said, "Put it back."

Mary, horizontal under one of my arms, said, "No."

"Put it back please."

"No."

I grabbed it and she squeezed and I prayed to the God of Stale Pastry that she wouldn't leave a mark.

"PUT IT BACK!"

"MIMI'S!! MIMI'S!!!"

"IT IS NOT MIMI'S!!"

I yanked the box free and put it back on the shelf. She righted herself, looked up at me, hair in eighteen different directions and shouted, "NOW MIMI'S SAD!!"

I heard some discrete snickers around me, but they were hard to pick up over the sound of all the guffaws as I threw my kid over my shoulder and made for the door.

Imagine Mary's delight - and mine - when we returned to the market a few days later and she found the pastry still there, in the same box, just like an old friend.

"Mimi's," she says, picking up the box and dropping it into her cart, chatting about old times.

Do you think they make danish play houses? Danish outfits, maybe? Little danish hats? Just like a Mr. Potato head only with coconut sprinkles.

Ah, well. It could have been so much worse. A side of pork really can't carry a hat.

Today in the closet under the eave I found:
half a fruit leather
Mary Poppins' hat
and the left shoe I've been looking for for a week

posted by Elizabeth at 4:23 p.m.

CHUBBY CHECKER
Wednesday, September 8, 2004

I was doing my monthly "crap sweep" of the office, where I basically take all the stuff that doesn't have a place, go through it, sort it, decide it doesn't have a place, and put it all back where it was, only more neatly.

In this process I found a jury summons. For September 1.

Oopsie.

I vaguely remember filling out the little cardy thingy and sending it back. As I scoured the notice I saw a small print caveat proviso doohickey that said they'd send a confirmation package ten days before the date.

Well, I know that never came. So how much trouble could I possibly be in?

After pressing all the right buttons and listening to the automated system I got a real person.

I could actually hear him frown as he looked at my record.

"You requested a change of court."

"That's right!" I remembered. "The one I was assigned is two hours away and I have to pay a sitter as it is."

"Okay. Um... you also checked off that you're a felon?"

"Er?" I mean, I've filled out a lot of forms in my life but I've never managed to accidentally create a criminal record for myself that way.

"And, um... are you Native American *and* Latin American?"

"I'm really really white. Like, I know Beach Boys lyrics."

"Yeah, looks like you tried to cross it out. Oh, no, that's *just a squiggly.*" Just a squiggly... wait a minute...

"Um. Does it look like, maybe, I dunno... a toddler or something... maybe drew on it?"

"Ahhh... yeah. Good hand eye coordination. She got the checks right in the box."

I could see it. Mary on her tummy, clutching a pen, little tongue stuck out. "Momma forgot to check THESE boxes..." Check, check. Check, check.

"You'll be glad to know the one thing you are not is American Samoan – what's she got against them, you suppose?"

"She's not a fan of capital S's. That's all."

"Oh, of course."

"No harm meant to American Samoans."

"Of course."

"Sir, you're not... hahaha... American Samoan perchance, are you?"

"No."

"Great, can I get my court reassignment?"

"Yes."

"Is this one of the funnier calls you've had lately?"

"It's not bad for a Native American Beach-Boy listening Latina felon who doesn't know how to use a calendar."

Okay, he didn't say that. But he did give me my new court date and I'm off the hook for ditching. How cool is that?

posted by Elizabeth at 1:32 p.m.

Conversations, Part I

Thursday, September 9, 2004

"Hey, El, remember when I set the trash can on fire?"

"Yeah. I remember that. We were on the phone and you had to be excused."

"Right. Fireplace ashes sometimes contain coals. It was an important lesson. Remember when I burned the rice and the fire department came?"

"Yup. I remember. They were nice, weren't they?"

"Oh. So nice. And Mary loved the truck. Remember the fried fish? Remember that?"

"When you set the kitchen wall on fire? Yeah. I remember that."

"Okay, well, lemme tell you about today. I woke up and the cats had crapped on the porch."

"Oh dear."

"Yeah. So I cleaned it up and hosed it down but it was so yucky. Then, the dog did it a few minutes later! SAME SPOT!! I was SO PISSED."

"Where do the flames come in?"

" ... so then, I put my oatmeal on the stove..."

"Here it comes."

"... and when I went back to the porch to clean up after the dog guess what?"

"Hmm?"

"Mary had taken off her diaper and *peed right there*. I am not making this up. My porch is like, some cosmic Pee Center of the Universe or something. Careful when you visit. Maybe we should take our coffee in the dining room."

"That's so totally nasty."

"Right. So I was cleaning. For the third time. Thinking how sad it is that this is my life, now, cleaning up the various stuff the beasties and the kid emit – and then I noticed smoke ..."

"Oatmeal?"

"How much does it suck that after all that, I didn't even get breakfast?"

posted by Elizabeth at 3:39 p.m.

What Happens When You Don't Listen to Auntie
Friday, September 10, 2004

I spent 30 minutes looking for my keys before I stopped to ask Mary.

"Mary. Do you know where Momma's keys are?"

(Thoughtful.) "Yeah."

"Oh," (not even sure she understood the question) "could you please tell me where?"

"Momma... kanikinananee... keys... baadeama... Mimi's bag."

"Mimi's bag?"

"Yeah."

Bag, bag... in the bedroom, on the floor, a plastic grocery bag. Inside, the controller to the Elmo train, three slices of apple, the doggie book... and my keys.

D'oh!

Today, Mare is feeling:

posted by Elizabeth at 6:14 p.m.

THE KITE
Thursday, September 16, 2004

Our neighbor Mr. Rainer brought us a kite.

I don't know where it came from – it was a bit tattered and had clearly been in someone's garage for a while. It was delta-shaped and yellow and orange and Mary loved it immediately.

"Let's go fly a kite!" she said, dragging it around the living room by its string. "Kite! Kite!"

We finally got motivated to haul all the kids to the beach, and we brought the kite with us. Miss Suzanne got the kite going while the kids watched. It caught some altitude immediately, and Mary squealed with joy when Miss Suzanne offered her the chance to hold the string.

It was a glorious sunny day, and that kite sparkled and shone as it pulled free from Mary's grasp and made for the sea like a white-legged senior in a bathing cap.

Miss Suzanne dove for the string in a desperate attempt to head off disaster. But the kite was gone, soaring along on a nice offshore breeze, the spool skipping along the waves below.

Mary stood at the shore, devastated.

"Mimi's sorry," she whispered. She burrowed her face into my shoulder. "Mimi's sad," she wept.

"I know, honey."

With Mary's birth I was welcomed back into the world of childhood and wonder – rediscovering the magic of fresh summer corn and boat rides, and how funny it is that a dog will chase a ball.

But I forgot about this part, that the inanimate feel like friends, and there are no little sorrows.

"Kite, all gone," she sobbed.

We stood at the water's edge and watched it until it was out of sight. I pondered the cosmic wonder that today my daughter first considered life and death, although she doesn't know it. Some little line was drawn across the unmarked canvas of her soul and I was there to see it.

The awesome responsibility of saying the right thing was making it hard to breathe. "Mary is sad," I said finally managed. "Mary is okay. Sad is okay. Kite is gone. Kite is okay."

In this world of mother and child, a two cent kite that sat in a garage for years came out to change us both forever, and was quickly gone.

Mary will never remember it. I'll never forget it.

posted by Elizabeth at 6:12 p.m.

Gluteus Minimus

Friday, September 17, 2004

Joseph is my new trainer.

Yes, he's hot.

He's a gorgeous African-American with a total BOD (yeah, duh) who is so great at saying, "Good job Elizabeth!" (Which, honestly, I really feel he should be doing at least once a set. I spend my day congratulating a two year old for being able to identify her own knees and no one pays me a penny.)

I have to remind myself when Joe and I are visiting that I did sixteen hours of natural labor.

Joe thinks it's tons of fun to get my heart rate up to a certain level ("In the zone" he says with puke-worthy enthusiasm) before he hooks me up to some godawful machine and forces me to contort myself in all sorts of funky ways while I breathe heavily and pray for relief.

Wow, yeah, that really is like labor.

If my breathing becomes too unburdened for Joe he makes me get back on the bike while he shouts, "Charge the fences!!" or is it, "Haul over the fence?" Maybe it's "Throw yourself at the fence" – whatever it is, it sure is motivating. Man do I want to go faster when he says that. Woo hoo.

I find myself thinking about Joe a lot during the day. Like whenever I have to bend over to pick something up. Or whenever my cute kid asks me to carry her up the stairs.

"Sure, honey, Mommy will carry you up the stairs just as soon as she picks her ass up off the floor. I think that's where I left it this morning when I dragged myself in here to get some coffee."

I said I wanted a J-Lo hiney and now we're working the glutes... charge those fences!

Glutes... gluten... bread... Hmmm, beer...

Anyway. My journey to Joe began a few weeks ago with the arrival of the Gym Dandy renewal notice in the mail. It came in a little thingy from the Community Center - a form to fill out for the class (please enclose a check); a form to renew Community Center membership (please note request for check); and an envelope (perfect size for your check).

That little pile of money suck sat there for a week. I just couldn't get around to it. I know that all the good mothers in the neighborhood take their children to Gym Dandy wearing their Mommy-and-Me Land's End outfits... but the thought of it just made me miserable.

Strike one: it's early in the morning. So I skip a lot. I skip a *lot*. (Sometimes, with other appointments in the day, it gets to the point that if we go to Gym Dandy there's no time to swing through the Starbucks drive-thru and we KNOW we can't have that.)

Strike two: I can't do insipid at 9:00 a.m.. I just can't. I can do insipid over cocktails, I can do it over coffee and meeting agendas... but insipid at 9:00 a.m. over munchkin-sized climbing equipment makes me want to curl into the fetal position and suck my thumb.

I was mulling all this over on a walk with Mary when I happened by the Body Shop. Behind a big window, people on machines were running helplessly toward the glass like sad little gerbils. I just knew I had to be one of them.

I met Joseph and we talked about how my body never really recovered from pregnancy. (Or "The Great Anatomy Migration of Ought Two".)

"I think it was the hormones," I said. "Or the morning sickness. It might have been the 200 doughnuts I ate, but let's not reach, okay?"

Something about being a mother makes you put your kid before all else. But the truth is, too much of that and the kid isn't getting what she needs most, which is you.

Sometimes, the trick is figuring out how to put yourself first so there's something for the kid's needs to be carried on. Getting me to the gym is better for Mary than getting her there.

But if I start dipping into her college fund for lattes, I'm counting on you to stop me.

posted by Elizabeth at 1:12 a.m.

Even in Australia...
Wednesday, September 22, 2004

When I woke up this morning, Mary had her fingers in my eye balls.

It was only 6 a.m. and I forgot to set the coffee pot last night. Cute Husband fell asleep in front of the television, so he wasn't there to take her downstairs. So I had to, and I could tell it was going to be a terrible horrible no good very bad day.

"Fruit bar?" Mary asked with hopeful blue eyes. Oh my God, I forgot to get fruit bar. She saw my face and said, "Apple??"

What the hell kind of mother doesn't keep a damn apple around?

"Mary... I got something even better for you. How about yogurt?? Huh, baby?"

She was totally humoring me. She sat in the chair with the yogurt and I fumbled with the coffee bag and spilled a bunch of it and while the dog was licking the grounds I thought, "Oh, man, that's really gonna suck very, very soon," but I was so desperate for coffee I didn't care. I just knew it was going to be a terrible horrible no good very bad day.

I got the coffee made and started the oatmeal but we only had a little left. I smothered Mary's in almonds and brup-up and figured that would hold her and it did – she liked hers so much she asked for mine and of course I gave it to her.

I have a lot of cleaning and organizing to do before Mary's big party Saturday so I let her watch *Winnie the Pooh* while I did laundry, washed floors, and tried to clean cat vomit out of Ducky's carpets. I know she's psyched she's letting us live here.

The table cloth sat in the dryer over night and now it looked like a piece of tin foil someone tried to reuse. Ducky has an ironing board from the late 1950s. I can deploy, but I cannot retract so I try not to iron if Cute Husband isn't around to make it all go away. Once it was down, I figured I'd watch silly Pooh get lost in the Hundred Acre Wood while I pressed every bow and pleat on Mary's party dress. I felt a swell of mother-pride that I got the blue frosting out of it after Cousin Ben's birthday party.

I laid the dress and the delicate white sweater flat so they would be ready for the big day.

"On! On!" Mary said. Well, I mean, I was the incompetent who blew the apple and the fruit bar thing am I really going to deny her this, too?

So she put the sweater on and I thought we were good, but no, she wanted the party dress, too, so that went on over the sweater (which was already over her regular clothes.)

I only half buttoned it, figuring she'd give it up soon, but she didn't and we went to the market like that. Little hobo.

Of course, I forgot my shopping list so I had to wing it. Mary was driving the little shopping cart car and making beeping noises while I tried like hell to remember what I was supposed to be getting. Thank God I remembered my *In Touch* magazine (all the gossip of People, half the price.) I think J-Lo and Marc Anthony may be on the skids, but don't quote me.

I got really excited when I saw a sign that said, "Mary Poppins available" and I thought, "Wow! For parties! That's so cool – wonder what she's doing Saturday?" but then I saw that the sign said, "Management Positions available" and I thought, "Thank God no one is inside my head because lots of people would be laughing at me" but now I've gone and told all of you, so what's the point?

Yes, I forgot the fruit bar.

Back home, the dog was chasing her own tail and terrorizing the cats. Pieces of shredded tennis ball littered the living room. She had a crazed look about her and I remembered the coffee thing and sent her outside for the rest of the afternoon. Not a squirrel in the neighborhood rested, let me tell you.

I bent over to pick up pieces of tennis ball and cracked my noggin on the front of the monster ironing board that was sitting there in the middle of nowhere. Within minutes I had a purple bruise on my forehead.

I spent a few minutes reading *In Touch* and planning my story.

"Mary was running, down the stairs, and this big, um, rock, was coming at her, and I dove... and rolled, and she was safe. But I bumped my head. More dip?"

Mary finished *Winnie the Pooh*. Then she watched *Mimi Hoppins*. Twice. Then it was Pooh again. It's a gorgeous day out and I'm singing, "The most wonderful thing about tiggers, is tiggers are wonderful things!" while I try out three or four different products to fade the color of regurgitated Meow Mix in carpet wool.

I'm supposed to go to the gym tonight but I think I'll stay home eat a pan of brownies and go to hell with myself.

Because bodacious bottoms need a break sometimes. Even in Australia.

Cute Husband came home and put the ironing board away with a flick of the wrist.

What-the-hell-ever law school boy.

posted by Elizabeth at 9:38 p.m.

T-Minus One Day Until the Toddler Party

Friday, September 24, 2004

It all would'a been different if Miss Suzanne hadn't gotten her ass bitten by a brown recluse spider.

We had set today aside for the planning and preparation for Mary's party. There were kiddie pools to fill, veggies to chop, floors to sweep, and general chaos to prepare for.

Miss Suzanne has been coming over to entertain Mary a few hours a week while I work in the office. She was due at 9:00 a.m. to keep an eye on Mary and help us out with some cleaning and organizing. 9:00 came and went and I figured she was running late. By ten, I thought maybe I had the time wrong. At 10:15 I cracked out the cell phone to call her and collected this message off my voicemail:

"Sorry about the party, a spider bit my ass. I'm on Vicodin, you're on your own." Or something to that effect.

Spider bites, apparently, can be very painful. I'm not sure how my child's beloved caregiver happened to come by one on her posterior, but if I get any details, I'll be sure to share.

In the meantime, I was left with a monster to-do list and a wired kid who still hasn't taken off that party hat. Cute Husband ~ bless his heart ~ decided to ditch school, and we broke the to-do list between us.

The first problem, of course, was the kiddie pool. Several weeks of unuse had turned it into a gigantic petri dish. We drained, we scrubbed, we negotiated placement.

The pool's regular home is on the deck. But that's where we're doing the grilling. Cute Husband just doesn't understand FLOW. Grill is adult country. Pool is kid country ~ we needed to get the pool out on the lawn with the climber.

The only problem with this plan is that we don't happen to have a garden hose.

"Whatever it was that bit Suzanne, I hope it was big," Cute Husband said, dutifully dragging his fifth bucketful of water from the kitchen, through the living room out the porch, down the stairs, to the pool.

"Hang in there, hon," I said. Mary had found a stash of party hats and was trying to put them all on her head at once like a freakishly confused Madonna. The dog was digging raw chicken scraps out of the trash.

I got the dog out of the kitchen and cleaned it all up.

I wandered back out into the dining room and stopped dead in my tracks.

"Good doggie," Mary said.

Seated loyally beside her, looking confused but very indulgent, Ginny was wearing a pink party hat. It was perfectly placed, with the rubber band behind her ears.

"Geewee hat! Party! Cake?"

"Cake's tomorrow."

"Okay," Mary shrugged obligingly.

"Maybe Ginny can take the hat off until the party?"

Ginny blinked hopefully.

"Um. No. Hat, on."

Nothing like a pink hat to turn a monosyllabic toddler into a tyrant.

Today, Mary is feeling:

ROYAL

WHEN THE DAY IS GREY AND ORDINARY...
Monday, September 27, 2004

You really don't understand magic until you are a parent, when you become a master magician beyond your wildest dreams. I thought this when I brought Mary down the stairs after her nap the day of her birthday party.

While she was sleeping, her parents and uncles and cousins had been hard at work. Grown men and women spent two hours hanging pink paper strips all over the house just because it would make a two-year-old happy. The result was spectacular – pink-coated banisters, pink streamers from the ceilings, pink cascading down the walls, punctuated by clusters of pink balloons

Mary had fallen asleep in her present from Aunt Emily – a fairy princess costume with layers of pink frilly twirly skirt. I dug around in a cloud of pink, trying to find her head.

"Wake up, baby girl," I whispered, lifting her out. I brought my daughter down the stairs and watched her face light up.

"Mimi's party!" she whispered reverently.

"Yes, sweetheart. Mimi's party."

She screwed her party hat to her head and squirmed out of my arms reaching for her yellow chair and the bright pink balloon tied to it. I loosened it for her and she grasped it and started to twirl. The Disney CD was playing and at that moment, "Jolly Holiday" came on. Mary held her balloon and twirled.

"It's a jolly holiday with Mary! Mary makes your heart so light! When the day is grey and ordinary, Mary makes the sun shine bright!"

Mary wasn't worried about whether anyone was having a good time, whether the food was good or the house was clean. She didn't care whether it was all too much or not enough. She really didn't care what anyone thought at all.

She just twirled there, all by herself, lost in the music and the magic of pink streamers and twirly skirts.

Whatever we think we're teaching our kids, they teach us so much more.

posted by Elizabeth at 9:06 a.m.

SUDDENLY NOT SO PORTABLE

Tuesday, September 28, 2004

When Mary was little, she came with us everywhere. We put her in the chest pack, popped a pacifier in, and off we went. She'd look around, watch the goings on, and generally just chill.

Not so much any more.

Yesterday, Cute Husband thought it would be fun to take Mary to class with him. We had a long talk about it, but he assured me that Mary would think it was fun and in the event that she couldn't hold out the whole hour, he'd be happy to leave. But she had a stack of quiet toys that she'll sit and play with at home, why wouldn't this work?

So off Mary totted to school with a couple of Barbies, a sippy of milk, and a soft alphabet book in her backpack. Daddy sat her on the floor and explained that Mary had to be quiet because... er... people were sleeping.

Mary nodded and set up her Barbies in a pleasant circle, put her milk beside her, and began to read to them in a hushed voice. The lecture commenced, Cute Husband dutifully took notes, and all looked well.

After a few minutes, Mary waved to get Daddy's attention. "DADA!" she said in a harsh whisper. "DADA!!" she said soberly. "Shhhh... *people are sleeping!!*"

"That's right, honey. Shhh... people are sleeping."

"Shhhhh..." she repeated to a smattering of giggles.

"Dada...mayamaneenee ababna *people are sleeping!*"

"Uh. Yeah. Time to go."

So twenty minutes after that little experiment began Mary was waving her goodbyes as she walked past the class toward the door. At the front row, just feet from the lecturer, Mary stopped short. "DADA!!" she said, pointing excitedly at a student holding a Starbucks cup, "Momma coffee!!"

That's right. A roomful of strangers laughed at me and I wasn't even there.

Today, I got the bright idea to take Mary to the mall. It used to work okay if she was in the stroller and we kept the visit short. But within minutes, Mary had formed a fast friendship with a discarded helium balloon. She amused herself by running ahead of me toting the balloon and squealing with maniacal laughter. Did I mention she was wearing her Easter hat?

"Look at that little girl with the balloon and the hat!" people kept saying.

"Um. Yeah. Keep looking at her. Can you, like, look at her for about twenty minutes while I hit the Gap?"

I thought our chances for survival would be better in a department store so we wandered over to Filene's. The balloon was a godsend because I could track her more easily with it. The balloon bopped along in and out of racks while I chased it, pausing here and there to grab a dress.

The balloon suddenly stopped moving, and for a minute I was worried.

Sticking out from under a tailored tweed suit was a round pink belly, little jeans, and bright pink boots. I could see the belly moving with inhalations, so that was good.

"BOO!! TA-DAAAAA!!!" Mary shouted, pushing the suit aside.

"Oh, so sneaky," I said. She took off running again, stopping dead in her tracks before a purse display.

"Oooo!!!" she said, grabbing a pink fuzzy clutch. "Mimi's bag!" and in a flash she was gone.

"Ahahahahahaha!! Mimi's bag, Mimi's bag!!" she squealed, making for the door in a flurry of pink and hats and trailing balloons.

"NO IT IS NOT MIMI'S BAG!"

"Mimi's turn! Mimi's party! PRESENTS!"

"No! Mimi's party was Saturday. UNHAND THE FUZZY PINK PURSE!"

"Nooooo... noooooo!!!! Mimi's!!!" she sobbed. Is there anything sadder than a kid in a hat clutching a pink purse and weeping?

Oh, yeah... a grown woman dragging the kid out of the store and looking longingly over her shoulder at her last glimpse of a shopping mall until 2016.

posted by Elizabeth at 2:01 p.m.

MARY, EMPRESS OF ALL SHE SURVEYS
Saturday, October 2, 2004

The in-laws are here for the weekend.

Mary: "Wabbit!"

Boppa: "Yes precious perfect that's a RABBIT!"

Gamma: "Perfect girl!"

Mary: "'raffe."

Gamma and Boppa: (wild we-just-won-the-pennant-and-it's-because-of-you applause) "YAAAAAAAY!!!! GIRAFFE!!!"

Mary: "More toast."

Gamma: "That's the last of the French toast, honey."

Mary: (pouts tragically)

Boppa: "Don't worry, Boppa will make more French toast!"

Mary: "Milk?"

Gamma: "Sure, baby!! More milk coming right up!"

Daddy: "Please? Mary?"

Mary: "No."

Daddy: "Er – did you just say no?"

Mary: "No, Dada. Go away. More milk, Gamma!"

Last night she had brie and ice cream for dinner.

Later today, she's going to Toys 'R' Us. Tomorrow I'm locking her in a room until she's thirty.

posted by Elizabeth at 9:04 a.m.

JUST CAN'T TAKE YOU TWO ANYWHERE

Monday, October 11, 2004

After DaMomma's Momma suggested a new outfit, the idea caught and I decided to throw caution to the wind and try, once again, to brave a shopping mall. That was how Cute Husband, Bored Toddler and I found ourselves in the Lord and Taylor shoe department.

"Aren't these *darling?*" ("Darling" is not a word I typically use in conversation, but there are certain fashion adjectives you're just allowed to use even if they sound dorky. It's a rule.)

"Um... can you walk in those?" Cute Husband asked incredulously.

"I labored in transition without pain relief for eight hours. I can do anything." I stood up and took a few confident strides in the snazzy lizard skin pumps.

"Ooo!!" Mary said. "On, on!"

She reached for a ped* and started yanking her sandals off. Little prodigy.

I helped her put on peds and she stepped reverently into the little pointy shoes.

"Shhhoooes!" she breathed. Cute Husband shuddered.

"Excuse me, she'll have to take those off," Nasty Saleswoman called to us from across the aisle.

"Oh? She's not hurting them or anything ..." Nasty Saleswoman glared unkindly at my child ~ who I might point out, was being perfectly quiet and sweet.

Until we yanked those shoes off.

So it was that the meltdown we had been avoiding commenced in earnest as the sassy shoes were removed and Mary was weepingly restored to her Stride Rites.

She and Cute Husband departed in a chaos of tears and peds and I was left in one of those maternal moral quandaries you read about so often. I did not want to give Nasty Saleswoman my business.

But man those shoes were cute.

So in the true spirit of the modern mother, I balanced devotion to child with devotion to fashion: I noted that the shoes were Nine West, dropped them like a hot diaper and booked it across the mall to the Nine West store where I found selfsame shoes in the appropriate size and promptly purchased them.

I wandered back out into the mall toward the sitting area where a very cute, albeit bored, man was seated on a bench with an extremely cute child perched on his lap.

Passersby were staring and even whispering. And no wonder. The child had a ped carefully stretched over her head.

"Oh my God what is our kid wearing?" I asked when I approached.

"What...? She was getting frustrated because it wouldn't go all the way up her leg, so I told her it was a hat –"

"Mimi's hat!!"

"– wasn't that smart thinking?"

"D'oh!"

posted by Elizabeth at 2:22 p.m.

*Peds are little pieces of panty hose you put over your feet when trying on shoes. They are also frequently worn as headgear by food service providers and rap stars.

An Update

Thursday, October 14, 2004

I've been seeing my friend Joseph for over a month now, and in the interest of good science, thought it was time to share some early results.

Update Number One: My ass still hurts.

Update Number Two: Joseph would like you to know that it's "shoot for the fences." Kind of Quixotic, actually. In a sad gerbil-in-the-glass, you'll-never-get-there kind of way.

Update Number Three: Last night while dressing for bed, I happened to catch a glimpse of myself in the mirror. I noticed the damndest thing: Right there, up above my battle-scarred belly button I saw the faintest shadow of ...stomach muscles.

Now, let's not go crazy or anything. We're not talking a six pack here, more like a few lumps in the water bed. But still. The last time I was that startled by my own anatomy a child was rolling around in it.

Update Number Four: I have to admit that I feel pangs of guilt when my friends tell me about the cool things their kids are doing that my kid is not ~ swimming lessons, Gym Dandy, music class. We can't afford these things right now because we opted to pay for Joseph instead.

Twice a week, I spend thirty minutes suspended from machines in excruciating contortions while a grown man inspires me with stories of non-existent fences. That doesn't sound like my ticket for the sanity train, I know, but something about it works. (C'mon, if someone suggested suspending yourself by your forearms six feet above ground while raising and lowering your legs in fifteen-second rotations, you'd pale, too.)

But just as important as the challenge is the cheerleading: it's really nice to have someone telling you that you can, and celebrating with you when you do. That's worth scheduling into your week.

Basically, we pay Joe to be my mother twice a week. My buff African-American Man-Mother.

Oh, and FYI, the J-Lo butt is coming along nicely. No. There will be no pictures.

posted by Elizabeth at 10:59 a.m.

Therapy was Going Nowhere
Sunday, October 17, 2004

This morning Mary was of the opinion that her doll-babies should not be left behind on our pancake run. Annabelle, the French Baby-Sized Freakishly Expensive one, and Gippy, Her Unfortunate Friend With One Misdirected Eyeball, were carefully strapped into Mary's car seat for the ride to the Paper Moon Café.

I was hoping to distract her on the disembarkation so she'd forget about her entourage. No such luck. She spotted her clear vinyl backpack on the floor and quickly dropped Gippy into it. Annabelle put up a bit more of a struggle. (See "French Baby-Sized," above – the French have startlingly large babies.)

"Nap, in backpack!" Mary said firmly.

"Annabelle needs to take a nap in the backpack?" (I am no longer capable of having a conversation where I don't repeat the other party's statements in a cheery monotone.)

"Yes," Mary said in her best *duh, Mother* tone. I carefully arranged Annabelle so her body was inside the plastic, but her head was peeking out, giving her a nice view and access to oxygen.

"NO, MOMMA, NAPPING!!"

Er, okay. I crammed Annabelle in the rest of the way, and zipped her in. When we were all through, she looked like something you might find in Hannibal Lecter's storage unit.

Satisfied, Mary pulled the bag onto her back and was off in the general direction of cancakes. Poor Annabelle's face, crammed in a jumble of arms and legs pressed against the plastic, seemed frozen in a cry for help.

A grey prison jump suit and a jar of fava beans, and we just may have Halloween covered.

posted by Elizabeth at 2:23 p.m.

Together, Apart
Sunday, October 17, 2004

It's nothing new, this struggle for balance between work and family. Women today have more options than ever before, and only the cynics are surprised that we're making more diverse choices than ever before.

For the last year, my work arrangement has been just dreamy. A couple of hours a week, my good friend Miss Suzanne watches the kid downstairs, while I work in the office upstairs. I'm still a stay at home mom, but I also work.

My little house of cards came crashing down this week when Miss Suzanne announced she was leaving us in favor of New Orleans. Whatever, crawfish po'boys.

So now I am seeking child care alternatives. This led me to the backyard of Miss Caitlin, a bright young woman with a degree in early childhood development. In three hour segments, little kids tear her home apart, grind paint and Play-Doh into her carpets, and generally exhaust themselves so their proper owners can take them home and put them down for nice long naps.

The biggest draw in that yard was a huge multi-colored plastic climbing gym that was at least three times the size of the one at home. The slide's platform stood at eye level. Mary grabbed on and tried to pull herself up.

"Stuck!" she announced a few seconds later, swinging from arms that just couldn't seem to get her up on to that platform.

"Pull harder, Mary," Miss Caitlin said. She wasn't unkind or harsh, just even. "You're-not-the-light-of-my-life" even.

"Stuck!" Mary said again.

"Keep pulling!"

She kept wriggling and pulling, and soon her body cleared that last grateful inch that put the balance of her weight on the platform. She grinned and I resisted the urge to give a "you-are-the-light-of-my-life" cheer.

"That pulling seemed to work for you, Mary," Miss Caitlin smiled. "That was a good trick." Mary went down the slide, ran around, and went back at the platform again. This little kid in pink overalls bore no resemblance to the baby who learned to walk a year ago today.

"So tell me what benefits your program specifically offers to the child of a stay at home mother?" I asked.

Miss Caitlin rattled off the statistics about socialization, and the benefits of group play and learning. "She's lucky that you're home with her," she said, "but getting out into the real world is good, too."

I get it.

My days as a lifeguard – the arrogance with which I relieved people of their children and took them off into the pool, or threw them off the diving board or taught them to swim alone in the deep end. That fierce little "You can't possibly know how I feel about this child" expression those mothers gave me as the universal response to my assertion that I had it all under control.

I get it now.

Getting it is a rite of passage, a wound of birth that never heals. I looked at Miss Caitlin and wished on her the blessed curse I knew had been wished on me a million times.

May you someday know just how hard it is.

We agreed to see Miss Caitlin next week and headed for home by way of the bakery to pick up Auntie B's cake. I had intended to let Mary have a cookie, but at the sight of the cake, her eyes widened and she requested a fork.

I selected a cupcake for her and added it to our bag instead, but it was too late. She was trotting to the seating area chirping, "Sit at the table. Fork, please, Momma?" I brought the cupcake and fork and sat beside her. A few bites in she discovered a purple sugar witch and chomped away at it happily.

"Danku, Momma," she said, with gigantic blue eyes and a chocolate smeared face. She stuck out her purple tongue and giggled. I laughed and leaned in and planted a smooch on her chocolaty lips, setting her giggling again.

My boss, the congressman, used to say that the mother/child relationship was the only one which God intended to become more separate over time.

Sometime in the last months, I stopped being the woman with a baby, and became the mother of a little kid.

Two people, mother and daughter, we make our way along – and slowly apart.

posted by Elizabeth at 7:36 a.m.

THE HAZARDS OF DAYCARE
Wednesday, October 20, 2004

Mary went for her trial session at Miss Caitlin's this morning.

Things did not start off well.

First of all, I was up really late watching the Sox last night and wouldn't you know it, today Mary decided to get up early. We all know how I feel about that.

Precious Perfect woke me by beating me about the face with her big plastic Shrek-and-Donkey cup holder. We don't use it to hold cups. She just likes to carry it around the house under her arm.

Next she brought me some playing cards and a fruit bar wrapper with ants on it. Please don't give me grief about my housekeeping.

When I'm up at 7:00, it takes me about an hour to feel totally awake. When I'm up at six thirty, it takes me about three hours.

So I can't tell you exactly what I did between 6:30 and 8:45, all I know is that suddenly we were late, we weren't dressed and I could only find one of her shoes.

Mary has a gazillion pairs of PJs but I think the Monster in the Laundry Room must'a got them because I haven't seen them in a while. So she kind of slept in her clothes. Her hair was all cockeyed and wild and she was wearing red leggings with a pink flowered top that had peanut butter on it.

On Sarah Jessica Parker, that's high fashion.

I decided Mary basically looked dressed, dug up a spare pair of shoes that don't really fit, crammed them on her feet and we were good to go.

We were finally in the car and headed for Miss Caitlin's. She swears it's only 12 minutes from my house to hers, but I've never made it in less than an hour. She's exquisitely competent with toddlers, but not so hot on directions.

The kids were headed to the back yard when we got there, so I screwed up my courage, nudged Mary forward and said, "Go on. Go play!"

She tromped off, a confident woman, while I cried like a clingy toddler.

The best thing about watching toddlers play is figuring out how they see the world. The first thing they all did was man the play strollers. Dillon put sticks and rocks into his. Caroline's stroller was empty, but she pushed it fast to catch up with Dillon.

Mary put all the babies in her stroller, tucked them in, then picked up a cell phone and started chit chatting excitedly while she rolled the babies along. Um. Yeah.

We stayed an hour, but it was enough to know that this was a good fit.

Pulling out of Miss Caitlin's driveway, I glanced at Mary in the mirror and said, "Did you have fun? Did you learn anything new?" Her response will forever remind me of all the things I simply cannot teach her.

With the excited look of the newly enlightened, Mary nodded, crammed her finger up her nostril and said knowingly, "Booger, Momma! *BOOGER!*"

Today, Mare is feeling:

A Princess, A Frog & Two Ghosts
Saturday, October 23, 2004

As Miss Suzanne and her son Robert prepare to depart for New Orleans, we have decided to commemorate their time with us with an honest-to-goodness sit down portrait. We met at the mall, and Mary donned her princess dress and Robert his frog costume.

Things started to go awry the minute Suzanne set Robert down in front of the fake evening sky backdrop. He realized he was expected to sit there alone, sprawled on his back and howled at the moon.

Our photographer was a Dippy Teen whose solution to toddler unhappiness was to shout, "LOOK AT ME I HAVE A PRETTY BEAR ON MY HEAD WANT TO SEE THE BEAR OH OH WHATS THAT NOISE, LOOKY OVER HERE AT ME!!" It was hard to hear Robert's screams over her consolations.

It was clear that if this picture were going to happen, Suzanne needed to be in it.

No mother taking her child to the mall after naps is dressed to be in a picture that will be displayed in a frame for all eternity.

Thank God that's not me, I thought, as I watched Suzanne grudgingly arrange her child to cover the ketchup stains he left on her shirt at lunch.

"Momma!!" Mary said.

D'oh!

Miss Suzanne smirked as I took my place next to her, Mary in my lap.

This was when Dippy Teen got a great idea.

If you don't want moms in the picture, just hide the moms. She brought out a big white sheet and dropped it over our heads.

So there we were, Suzanne and I, snuggled under the sheet together while Dippy Teen shouted, "MOM RAISE ROBERT HIGHER! MOM, BRING MARY CLOSER IN!! CLOSER TOGETHER, MOMS! CLOSER!" Soon, we were cheek-to-cheek.

Suzanne, bless her heart, was still very much in the game. "Robert, are you going to kiss Mary?" she coached from under the sheet.

"Hug Robert, Mary!" I pitched in. "Go on."

After we got the kids mostly assembled we met with the photographer to go over the digital proofs and make our order. You know, it's funny: after all that, it really did look like a princess and a frog sitting in the laps of two people who inexplicably had a sheet over their heads.

Dippy Teen hadn't considered a few aesthetic problems. First of all, I am a good deal shorter than Miss Suzanne. So no matter how close we got, we couldn't make up for the half-a-foot distance between where I end and she does. Second, the shot was wide enough to reveal Mary sitting on khaki and Robert sitting on jeans. Third, and perhaps most significant, our arms were clearly visible around the waists of our respective children.

I suppose on some level, it really is more descriptive of our time together than a prim portrait would be. Two moms taking care of kids and making life work have to improvise, and sometimes it gets messy.

Of course, no one looking at this picture on my dresser is going to say, "Wow, look at that great mother partnership!" they're going to say, "Why do you two have a sheet over your heads?"

The simple answer to that, my friends, is that we were too dumb to say no.

posted by Elizabeth at 8:54 a.m.

Bitter Betrayal
Tuesday, October 26, 2004

It's Tuesday, and Joseph and I are visiting. I am very very tired. The Sox have come back against the Yankees, victory is just over the hill and I just know if I don't watch every minute of every game our hopes will be crushed again. So I watch. Oh, how I watch. THE FREAKING BLIMP GAVE UP AT 1:00 A.M. AND I WAS STILL WATCHING!

"Okay, Elizabeth, hop up on that scale for me, please."

"You know, that's just what I wanted to do. Hop. On a scale. Woo. Hoo."

[THIS PORTION CENSORED]

"Boy that was some fun scale hopping, let's do some machines for even more fun."

"Actually, I want you to come over here, and put on the boxing gloves." I put them on, he had me lie on my back, and I started punching alternating hands while doing sit ups.

I think Joe's theory is to exhaust me past the point of being a wise ass. That's when he knows he's done his job.

"This is... so much... fun..." I puffed.

"FASTER!! Elizabeth! Not a fence is safe tonight!"

"Slaughter... those ... f – "

" – ENCES!! That's right! That's the attitude I want."

"Hey, great shirt," I puffed.

It featured an image of a sweet young boy in a Red Sox outfit with his middle finger extended. The caption read, "Who's your Daddy, now??"

"Thanks," Joe said. "I lost a bet."

"Yeah, but how could you have ... oh no." With horror, it dawned.

All this time we'd spent together, not a hint. Not a clue. There was a tense pause while Joseph studied my face for signs of rejection or disapproval.

"AHAHAHAHAHAHHA!!" I laughed. "Are you CRYYYYYING Yankee boy?"

"FASTER!" he demanded.

"AHAHAHAHAHA ... *saaad* Yankees!! I've been dying to taunt one in person and here you were all this time! You lost! Hee hee!!"

He made me do fifteen more and I just didn't care.

"AHAHAHAHA! Yankee boy!!"

"Hey," I said a little while later, sipping water after a fun few minutes swearing at a stationary bike. "Serious for a moment – I gotta skip Thursday, I have a chick date."

"A what?"

"That's when two moms get together, eat, and analyze the various emotional motivations of everyone in our lives without anyone glazing over or turning on the game."

"Where are you going?" he asked casually.

"Legal Seafood."

"What do you plan on eating?" *Danger, Will Robinson, DANGER!* A cool hush settled as Joe and I locked gazes. I said:

"Butter. Deep fried in hydrogenated oil. Topped with ultra-processed corn syrup."

"Back. On. That. Bike."

I can't even believe I'm paying this guy. Who knows where my check goes? Blue and white striped outfits or something... I shudder to think.

posted by Elizabeth at 8:18 p.m.

LOSING AN AUDI ON A THURSDAY NIGHT
Friday, October 29, 2004

It's funny, after I was married I understood the value of keeping up with my girlfriends and going out without the husband once in a while. But somehow, after Mary was born, I forgot. Cute Husband and I both take for granted that he has beers with friends after class, or goes to receptions and things at the law school. I, on the other hand, have not been to a social event outside the presence of my daughter or husband in over two years.

This was the scene as I prepared for my date:

Cute Husband: "Wow, is that the new outfit your mom got you?"

Me: "Yes. El and I agreed no house pants. We have to look cute."

Cute Husband: "You do look cute."

Me: "I totally do, don't I?"

Cute Husband: "Are you sure you're meeting Ellie?"

Me: "Huh?"

Cute Husband: "You're not, like, hooking up with Joe or anything are you?"

Me: "Oh my God. I have to do this more often."

Meanwhile, at El's house:

Ellie's Husband: "Hey, the kid is shouting 'chicken nuggets and red dip,' what does that mean? Wow. You look hot."

Ellie: "I totally do."

Husband: "You're like dressed up. And stuff. I mean. Just to see Elizabeth?"

Ellie: "Yes."

Husband: "Just her? No one else? I mean... no... like, man?"

Ellie: "Oh. Honey. That is so cute. FYI 'chicken nuggets' means 'chicken nuggets' and 'red dip' means 'ketchup.' Don't wait up for me."

At the restaurant we giggled over martinis and appetizers and continued our giggling through plates of wild salmon. We decided to take El's car to the theater and come back for mine after. We walked out to section 1:7 of the parking lot, where Ellie had left the Audi.

The leather-interior-no-Cheerios-ground-into-the-seat Audi. The dear-God-it-was-right-here Audi.

Ellie's Husband's fabulous corporate car was... gone.

For twenty minutes, we went up and down the rows of section 1:7, looking for the silver Audi with black runners on the roof. We played, "Where did you last have the nice automobile" and Ellie kept shaking her head and muttering sorrowfully.

Before calling the cops, Ellie relented to one last check, one section over, just to be sure.

"Um, El... is that your...?" I pointed to a silver Audi wagon with runners on the top. In section 1:8

"Just get in the damn car," she said, pushing her key fob to unlock.

We were late, so when we got there I said, "You're on tickets, I'm on snacks – " before taking off in my cute shoes that hurt like the dickens but are *sooo* worth it. The man at the door asked for my ticket stub and I threw him a smile.

"Silly, I'm on snacks, *she's* on tickets!" I breezed by unchallenged.

I still got it, baby.

At the counter I ordered Diet Cokes and popcorn and threw in a bag of Sour Patch kids. We snickered our way into the theater, stumbling over poor innocents and spilling popcorn in our quest for The Perfect Seat.

Ellie sipped her drink, tasted a Sour Patch Kid and scowled. "That. Tastes. Like acid reflux."

I spit Diet Coke out my nose.

Being a mother lets you back into the secret world of childhood: through your kids you once again experience the magic you'd almost forgotten about. Your enjoyment, though intense, is vicarious. And your burdens are much greater.

Something about losing an Audi in a mall parking lot made me feel like a kid again, like someone who could afford a little irresponsibility, who had enough time to spare that she could go out with a friend.

One woman walks into labor and delivery, and a different woman walks out. I think the road back to finding ourselves is far longer than we're ever told.

Lose an Audi, find your way. Not bad for a Thursday night.

posted by Elizabeth at 10:25 a.m.

Okay, Whose Bright Idea Was It?

Monday, November 1, 2004

I want to know whose bright idea it was to have Daylight Savings come Halloween weekend, on the heels of the Red Sox win, right before the elections?

Surely not a mother's.

Here's what I got: I haven't had a good night's sleep in eleven games and a parade. I am in possession of a wired, sugar-high kid who doesn't understand that going door to door in a costume this morning won't have the same effect that it did last night. At 5:00 a.m. she woke me by cramming two thumbs in my eyeballs and whispering: "No talking Mimi's *asleeping!*" followed by a long pause and, "Momma... trick or treat??"

Naptime was one gigantic Rage Against the Machine – she stomped her feet against the wall for an hour chanting, "No baby no sleeping!! No baby no sleeping!!"

SEND HELP. Or just a martini. And an Elmo video, and like, a big chair with Velcro arms I can secure her into.

Mary is feeling:

posted by Elizabeth at 1:30 p.m.

No Baby, No Sleeping

Friday, November 5, 2004

At the newborn phase everyone tells you to sleep when the baby sleeps. HA! Then when do you shower, huh, pal?? How about eat a meal, or throw in some laundry, or have that great crawl-in-the-corner-and-suck-your-thumb moment you've been promising yourself?!

So you pretty much don't sleep the first year, and then the second year, the naps become sort of predictable and the nighttime routine kind of reliable and suddenly you have a life again.

If you are like many of my friends, that's how you end up pregnant and back in the newborn phase.

One thing about kid sleep that I discovered is counter-intuitive: It simply doesn't follow that if you put a child to bed later, the child will wake up later. What she'll do is wake up earlier, and crankier, and then go on a nap strike.

This was the case following the Red Sox games, Halloween, and the end of Daylight Savings Time. After days of funky naps and weird bed times, Mary had become an elevated life form that no longer required sleep. A life form that protested oppression by my lower life form.

"NO BAYBEEEE NO SLEEEEPING!!" Mary shouted at naptime, stomping her feet against the wall above her crib. "NOOOOO BAYBEEEE NOOOOO SLEEEEPING!!"

She carried on like that for an hour and didn't sleep.

That night she refused to take off her pink princess dress. She was convinced that wearing it was the key to having complete strangers hand her candy and she didn't want to be unprepared. So we put her to bed in it, and of course, she was in our bed in no time and I was trying to negotiate sleeping next to six layers of puffy tulle.

Yes. Even in her sleep, she strongly objected to its removal.

By the end of the week, my definition of time had utterly changed. "9:15 a.m." was now "T-Minus three hours, forty five minutes 'till naptime."

Whoever invented Daylight Savings, I'm gonna find him, and I'm gonna send him a marching band. To his home. A large one. At, say, T-minus eight hours 'till naptime.

posted by Elizabeth at 7:46 p.m.

It's All Just Life

I was strolling the grocery aisles, chatting on my cell phone.

This is an obnoxious practice, I get that. Okay, honestly, I only half get it. I get that a person who is on her cell phone isn't exactly paying the best of attention to what's going on around her (which is how Klepto the Kid lifted a yellow bell pepper to munch on while we worked). But honestly – it's rude to listen in to other people's conversations anyway, so how rude can it be not to provide the other half to listen in on? You know?

So I was going down the cereal aisle carrying on my fair share of conversation ("No, honey, our family doesn't eat Lucky Charms; – Ratia, did you just say your husband said he'd *let* you work if you wanted to – ?") when I happened to notice my high school college admissions counselor standing across the aisle from me.

My first reaction, of course, was to check my fly. I stopped my hand midway across my abdomen. *No! It's the first sign of weakness! Check your zipper and she'll know she still has you!!*

I glanced away from her.

"Oh, really, Ratia? Ahahahah... that's so funny," I said in a casual, yet elegant, look-what-I've-done-with-my-life voice.

You were ten years worth of students ago. She's not going to recognize you. And even if she does, you're on the phone; she's not going to try to talk to you.

"Elizabeth?"

D'oh!

"Hmm? Oh! – " (*It's you! And your name is...?*) "– Robin!" ("Call me Robin. We're pals. Even if your SAT score made me laugh so hard I was revisited by 18 years post-partum incontinence.")

We all have our Robins.

"Robin" was a writer. And didn't think I should be one. "Everyone wants to write the great American novel," she told me. "You need real goals – ones *you*" (such gentle emphasis) "can achieve."

It was Robin who told me not to apply to Johns Hopkins, Robin who said I would embarrass myself doing it without her support. When I graduated from Hopkins with honors, I wanted to drop her a note and let her know. When I got my first job, and my first quote in a major newspaper, I wanted to send Robin clips. Some day, my people would call her to remind her she had no people.

We all have our Robins.

In all the times I imagined my triumphant telling off of Robin, I never considered what it would be like to just run into her in a grocery store one day.

The truth is, it wasn't like much at all.

"Um, this is my daughter," I said. She nodded. "So ... are you still working at the school?"

"Yeah," she said. "... probably never leave," she added with a dry laugh. We blinked at each other a few times.

I almost told her. Rattled off my resume, gave her the press secretary treatment, showed her what a powerhouse professional I was, even in old jeans at the market with my kid. I wanted to tell her about my brave choice to stay home with the baby; how happy and proud that made me, and that I didn't do it because I didn't have options.

But I realized it just didn't matter.

Writer, college counselor, or Momma to a bell-pepper spewing klepto, it's all just life. I am what I am and I don't owe anyone any explanations; for good reasons or bad ones.

"Good to see you," I said.

"You too," she said.

I turned away, laughing at all the things I'd ever wanted to say to her, and thanking sweet merciful Joseph that my backside was so darned worth looking at.

posted by Elizabeth at 9:04 a.m.

THREE BOOTHS, NINE CLOTH NAPKINS
AND A 33% TIP

Monday, November 15, 2004

It is possible to go out to eat with a toddler. You just have to tip more.

After a long day cooped up in the house due to snow, we decided to treat ourselves to Chinese food. (Rookie mistake. You don't take a toddler who's been cooped up inside all day to a restaurant.) We were led to a booth, we made our orders, and the waiter brought us a plastic basket of stale hoagie rolls.

Are Americans really that addicted to white carbs that Chinese restaurants feel the need to ply us with stale cafeteria bread while we wait for our kung pao?

Mary immediately started opening butter packets.

"Please make the bread disappear," I muttered to Cute Husband out of the corner of my mouth.

"Er. *Okay.*" He picked up the basket and set it on the bench next to him, in full view of our child, whose eyesight, as far as I know, is excellent.

She peered under the table and said, "Bread, Daddy?"

I threw him a look, he threw me one back, thought quickly and said, "MARY LOOK AT THE PANDA!" while he darted the bread behind his back to the empty booth behind him. Mary nodded at the print of a panda eating some bamboo.

"Panda," she agreed. "Where's the bread?" She stood up on the seat and leaned, overturning a water glass and soaking the nice paper Chinese astrology placemats.

We raided the empty booth for more cloth napkins.

Just then, the waiter arrived bearing a second basket of rolls. I thanked him while Mary opened some more butter pats.

"Here, put this in your pocket," I said thrusting a stale hoagie at my husband.

"Huh?"

"*Please!*" I hissed. "I don't want to hurt his feelings. I want him to think we ate some."

"Liz, there's a basket of rolls on the seat behind me... he's gonna know!"

How many rolls would fit in his pocket, I wonder?

Mary put her spoon in the dumpling sauce, spilling half of it over the table. The place-mats were now wet AND sticky.

While I tried to clean up, Cute Husband took Mary on a walk over to see the gigantic fish tanks. That was perfect until the food came and he suggested to Mary it was time to go back to the table. She wrinkled her nose up and threatened to scream.

I so wanted to join her.

There was an empty table next to the tank, so we grabbed it and Cute Husband and Grumpy Waiter started fire brigading our things over.

We were still waiting for the rice for Cute Husband's egg foo yung ("It'll be a while, all the waiters want a chance to spit in it") when Mary in one spectacular move put her foot down on the table and sent egg drop soup flying over everything.

We tried to hide the soupy napkins when the waiter came. He totally saw.

The bill came to $30. We tipped ten.

Today, Mare is feeling:

BOTTLED-UP

posted by Elizabeth at 10:28 p.m.

No More Ziti!

Tuesday, November 30, 2004

This is what I get for trying to be cool like Miss Karin.

Karin is crafty. In mother terms, this does not mean sneaky. It means that she actually gets motivated to have her kid paint egg cartons and glue stuff on paper plates.

Miss Karin does, however, have a slight obsession with ziti garlands. She knows it's a problem.

Daughter Emma likes to paint, and prefers the raw canvas of her naked body. So Karin spends a lot of time painting ziti and saying, "Emma, wouldn't it be great to hang this on the tree? Huh, honey?" Emma is too busy coating her arms in green and brown to care much one way or the other.

So I thought I'd be cool like Karin and we'd paint ziti. Cracked out the paint, the brushes, covered the place in newspaper, and told my little Monet to have at, make me an artwork.

Thirty minutes later I was putting the finishing touches on my fifth little ziti in perfect purple while Mary experimented with how much play dough she could ram into a Barbie shoe.

After the ziti dried, I strung them.

"Look, honey! A necklace!" I said.

"Uh-huh."

"Want to wear it?"

"No."

Right. Whatever.

I hung it over the edge of her chair where it remained for about a week.

Then last night I came into the room to find a cloud of colored ziti fragments spread out on the floor, the dog crunching away.

Mary looked soberly at me for a full ten seconds before she giggled.

"Is the dog eating ziti?"

"Ziti necklace," Mary confirmed.

The dog stopped crunching and swallowed.

"Gin. WHY?? Why are you eating ziti?"

As I talked, Mary absently tossed the dog one last sharp sliver of dried pasta, lovingly dabbed in fuchsia by me.

"Here Ginny, eat."

Ginny didn't move.

"EAT!!" Mary shrieked.

Ginny shrugged gamely and began crunching.

This time Mary looked sober a full fifteen seconds before giggling.

Mary is feeling:

posted by Elizabeth at 1:39 p.m.

TWICE THE FUN
Wednesday, December 1, 2004

One way to actually get some shopping done with a toddler is to hook up with another Mom so you can tag-team the kids. The benefit is twice the parental coverage; the cost is twice the chaos. El and I met at Wal-Mart with the girls for a little holiday preparation shopping.

The first problem was that freaking Santa is freaking everywhere.

"DANTA!! DANTA!!" my kid shouted, pointing to a shimmying plastic monstrosity blaring a staticky version of *Jingle Bells*.

"Danta?" asked Greta. (Her mother, apparently, thought maybe December should come before any mention of Santa Claus. Whatever, El.)

"Danta daindeer crimis twee pesents," Mary informed her. " – affer write da note."

They blinked at each other for a few seconds of complete non-understanding before Mary shrugged and dug her paws into Greta's bag of pretzels.

We hit the pet aisle for some accessories for Harry the Fish, whom Ellie thinks may be depressed for a lack of stimulation. His predecessors – Harry 1 and Harry 2 – were quite literally stimulated to death. "Fish tickling" was a popular occupation in which the girls crammed their fists into the tank squealing, "TICKLE, TICKLE, HARRY!" Harry 2 was the victim of "Bored? Let's go feed Harry!" being said a few too many times in his household.

That was when the kids learned that sometimes after a play date Harry likes to float on top of the water with his eyes bugged out and it's best to just turn off the lights and close the door when this happens.

The current Harry is looking a little down in the dumps and Ellie thinks some nice plastic greenery will cheer him up. She also picked up some smaller food pellets she thought more suited to Harry Whom We'd Like Not to Kill with Oversized Pellets Just When We've Gotten Past Tickling and Overfeeding.

I got some shelving systems, Ellie picked up some cute outfits, and pretty soon we were wheeling two loaded carts over to checkout.

I went first at the checkout, leaving Ellie to watch the kids. As I paid, I was vaguely aware of the two of them chasing each other, squealing, around a post. After my goods were loaded I went to relieve El.

"How'd it go?" I asked.

"Well, you can tell Mary has the dancing Elmo at home," she said, pointing to a wall of gyrating puppets. Mary had gone down the row and activated each one, creating a chorus line of high-pitched baby-talking red beasts singing the YMCA song.

Now I know what ABBA saw on acid.

Ellie got over to the checkout while I explained to the girls it was time to go, and no, the box of yellow smiley balloons on sticks was not coming with us.

"If you come now, you may each have a balloon," I said, digging into my pockets for spare change. Now the girls were sort of heading in the right direction, Ellie was all paid up and ready to go and all I had to do was pay for two balloons and we were outta there.

I was milliseconds too slow.

Mary had found a couple more of those balloons and was sprinting toward sporting goods shouting, "NOT YOURS!!" at the top of her lungs. Greta, not to be undone, tore off in the other direction and suddenly we were about six people understaffed. Ellie and I launched into warp speed, gathering kids, tucking balloons behind candy displays, pulling up pants, gathering packages and cajoling the whole mess toward the door.

"PLEASE TAKE MY MONEY!" I said, thrusting what I was sure was at least a dollar too much at the cashier.

"I have to ring it up," she said. I stared in exasperation.

"I... just... want to do the right thing!!" Ellie wailed.

It all worked out in the end. We got our stuff out to our cars, got our kids loaded, and headed for home. I bet Ellie's ride was just like mine: turns out the smiley balloon pops off the end of the stick very easily.

"Momma fix? Momma fix? Momma fix Momma fix Momma fix..."

Damndest thing how we can't seem to find that balloon now.

posted by Elizabeth at 7:00 a.m.

AM I ALL ALONE HERE?

Wednesday, December 15, 2004

Mary is visiting the Aunties.

"Aunchie mwakanakaneeki toas peabudder peas?"

"I'm sorry, honey, what was that?" (a sidelong glance at Da Momma)

"*Toast. Peanut butter,*" hisses Da Momma.

"Why sure, honey, let's make you some toast with peanut butter."

"Miwk pease?"

"*Milk.*"

"All right, and some milk."

"Wook piggy's faffing!"

"*Pig. Laughing.*"

"Yes, sweet girl, that piggy's laughing."

"Aunchie, booka nikinumna aganeepokie?"

"*Beats the hell out of me.*"

"Well, that's right, precious girl, thank you for sharing that with us."

"You're welcome, Aunchie."

posted by Elizabeth at 9:43 a.m.

A Lesson on Orange Juice

December 20, 2004

When I started this blog I swore a Super-Sacred-Golden Potty Vow – there would be no ever-so-charming poop stories.

However, motherhood is a learning curve, and we all have to share data in the interests of the common good. So this is really more Public Service announcement than Gratuitous Personal Commentary.

I do this for you.

Mary and I had gone with my aunt to this ancient ski shop nestled in the mountains of the Berkshires. I was admiring silk long underwear and – I kid you not – mink ear muffs, when Mary excused herself and retired to the privacy of a small dressing booth.

At this stage of the game, that means she needs a Moment. That kind of Moment.

The door, thankfully, was not self-locking, so after a few moments of silence, I poked my head in.

"Be right back!!" she said, slamming the door on me.

"Honey, time to go."

"No."

"Momma wants to go get some apple cider, want to go?"

She opened the door just wide enough to fulfill her desire to slam it in my face again.

"Lamby, I'm going to go get some apple cider, okay? – I'll be right back."

"COMING! COMING WITH YOU!" She opened the door and flew into my arms.

That was when I began to suspect that something was amiss in the general direction of her southerly pole.

"Um. Let's go get you a diaper change, okay, hon?"

We managed to find our way into the tiniest bathroom in all the ancient mountain ski shops in all the Universe: we had to embrace just to get the door closed.

My bulky parka radically impacted my mobility and magnified the significant rise in body temperature I was beginning to experience. Mary's layers further complicated matters: I had to dig through snow pants, jeans, leggings and long underwear to uncover a horror the likes of which has never been described in print before.

And shan't be today.

Suffice to say I had given Mary her first (and last) glass of orange juice this morning and the result was both copious and viscous – it stuck to her pants, my hands, and in an unfortunate moment of absent mindedness, to a wisp of hair I was trying to brush out of my eyes.

The key to this sort of situation is several deep breaths.

Not in that room.

My half-naked baby stood there very patiently while I dug around the grimy shelf next to the toilet for something – ANYTHING – that might help. I found a large box of plastic garbage bags and grabbed two. I immediately bagged the offending diaper, twisting inches of extra plastic into a heap, feeling first vague guilt about the landfill thing followed by a moment's pause as I contemplated the fact that some day, hundreds of years from now, some archeologist might consider this quite a find.

I dropped that bomb into the second garbage bag and then sat back and thought long and hard about my next move. There was still work to be done.

"Silly poop!" Mary snickered.

"Lean on my shoulders, babe," I said, reaching for the wipes. She gamely did as I asked, leaning in close and looking at me soberly.

"Siiiiilly poop! Don't touchit. Icky."

"I'll bear that in mind," I laughed. It was infectious – Mary snickered harder, and then so did I, which put her into guffaws.

My aunt, outside the door, knocked tentatively.

"I have to pee," she said. "Really, really badly. Oh. And the store is closed."

Ah. Yes. I used to close bars. Now this.

"It's going to be just a minute," I called through the door. Mary gave me a giant conspiratorial grin.

"Hey Mare? – you're tons of fun."

"Hi, Momma!" she said, kissing my nose.

I've bonded over some crazy stuff before.

But nothing quite this viscous.

posted by Elizabeth at 11:35 a.m.

CHRISTMAS CONVERSATION
Friday, December 24, 2004

Cute Husband: "I really don't know how it happened."

Damomma: "I know."

Cute Husband: "We weren't going to overdo it ... remember? Just a few gifts."

Damomma: "I think that pile is bigger than Mary."

Cute Husband: "Honey, it's bigger than the tree."

Damomma: "In fairness, it wasn't all us."

Cute Husband: "No. It was Santa."

Damomma: "Right. Oh, hey, while I'm thinking of it can we lose that book? Santa Claus is Coming to Town?"

Cute Husband: "But she loves that book!"

Damomma: "Oh, she's two. She loves empty toothpaste tubes."

Cute Husband: "What's Santa done to offend?"

Damomma: "It's not Santa, it's the message. 'Better be good, better not shout ...' Santa's love is unconditional. I don't even want to go there with her."

Cute Husband: "But she loves that book."

Damomma: "No, really, Mary and I had a huge discussion about it." (Momma: "Santa loves all the little children Mary. Black and white, and really ill-behaved ones who run around restaurants screaming while their parents do nothing. They get presents, too. Probably more since their parents obviously have a hard time saying no. So don't you believe that crap about behavior, okay?" Mary: "Candy cane, pwease?")

Cute Husband: "She likes the illustrations. Maybe we can tell her that some people think that – "

Damomma: "No, really, I hate that book. I'll just make it disappear and you won't remember, either."

Cute Husband: "I so totally will."

Damomma: "You so totally won't."

Cute Husband: "Keep talking like this and there's no way I'll forget."

Damomma: "Hey, husband, look!! CANDY CANE!!"

Cute Husband: "Oh, cool!! CANDY CANES!   Hey. Wait. I still haven't forgotten you know."

Damomma: "Of course not. I understand."

Today, Mare is feeling:

posted by Elizabeth at 10:54 a.m.

MARY PRINCESS AND HAPPY NEW BEAR

Saturday, December 25, 2004

The real reason for the lights:

Holiday lights are excruciatingly well-planned. At a time when roads are packed with wired, sleep-deprived children strapped into car seats for the umpteenth hour, the good people of the world gave us parents an out.

"WAAAAAAAAAAA!!!"

"Look, Mare, LIGHTS!!"

"Oh."

"Santa!! On the roof!! Oh, and look at that one! Sixteen colors on one tree! WOW!!"

"WOW Momma!! WOW!"

Long, agonizingly light-free block.

"MARE LOOK!!! OH MY GOODNESS IT'S A TRAFFIC LIGHT IN RED YELLOW AND GREEN OH WOW HAVE YOU EVER SEEN ANYTHING SO WONDERFUL MERRY CHRISTMAS!!!"

"May-we crimis!! May-we crimis!!"

###

CHRISTMAS CONVERSATION, PART II

"Mare? These are from Aunt Emily and Uncle Terry. Want to open them?"

"Hehehehehehehehe!!!"

"Mare... honey?"

"Hehehehehehehehe!!!"

"Oh no. We lost her. It's all over. MARE??? CAN YOU HEAR ME???"

"Hehehehehe... he... hehehehehehehe!"

"That's it. Stick a fork in her, she's done... guess I'll just open the last of these for her and put them away. Although, you know, what we should really do is put them in the attic, wrapped."

"She won't want these next year."

"Right. But there's no way our second kid is going to get anything like this so his or her only hope is if we stop ourselves now."

"Right. You open the ones on the left; I'll open the ones on the right?"

"Sweet."

Mary is feeling:

posted by Elizabeth at 7:38 p.m.

THE MATERNAL WOUND

This entry was written December 27, 2004, after tsunamis devastated portions of south Asia.

We're late getting back from my mother's, traffic is heavy, and Mary is freaking.

"Frooooooot baaarr!" she wails from her car seat. "Pweeeeeeease!"

Days of eating badly have caught up – she's asking for the whole grain breakfast bars that are our Old Reliable: nutritious, always in the backpack, and always palatable to Mary.

Unfortunately, I just don't have any on me.

"It's okay, honey." I have forced my voice to drop two registers – it calms us both. "It's okay. See that exit? That's where Whole Foods is. We'll stop there." I talk her through the exit, past two intersections, and point to the green Whole Foods sign.

"See that? Baby? We'll pop right in there and get your fruit bar." She's whimpering a little, and sniffling, but sun is peeking through the clouds: she knows there's a whole wall of fruit bar boxes in there and we'll pick up a couple of each.

Pulling into the crowded, slushy parking lot packed with grumpy shoppers it hits me: All over Southeast Asia tonight, mothers are frantic. The babies that weren't washed away are hungry and thirsty. Their parents would do anything in their power to stop it. The utter horror is that there's nothing they can do.

Before, I cared on an intellectual level about the suffering of the world. Now I feed my child with an agony of gratitude: oh God those poor mothers whose children suffer. Those poor children.

We have to make it better. I don't want to hear about the politics of who helped whom or what we can afford or whether it's really our job.

We can afford it. As long as our children eat and theirs don't, it is our job.

posted by Elizabeth at 5:37 p.m.

A Dramatic Reading

Thursday, January 6, 2005

After you read a book a few gazillion times, you stop actually reading, and just tell the story in your own words.

Momma's version:
"Oh, see, here's Princess Belle who is so beautiful, but so very smart and strong she doesn't take any crap off anyone... okay, so her Dad takes his invention to the fair, and he gets in trouble, and of course Belle helps because that's what you do when someone is sad or sick, you help, right Mare? So she helps, and then Beast, well, Beast was angry. It's okay to be angry, right, Mare? It's not scary, he's just angry, and Belle is telling him to express it better. Okay, so he gets hurt, and Belle helps, again, 'cause that's what we do. And then... oh... look at the pretty dress! Doesn't Belle look lovely? She and Beast are dancing! And then here, these villagers are angry, and Belle speaks to them in a calm voice about how important it is to think before you act and that fear is not a good reason to do something... (skipping some pages) LOOK MARE!! Belle and Beast are KISSING!! The End."

And then we have Daddy:
"Okay, so there's this handsome dude and he pisses off the ugly old lady and she turns him into an ugly dude. Here's Belle. She sings and stuff and she likes books and the villagers hate her except for Gaston who wants to marry her, but that's just bullshit, you stay away from guys. Okay, so her dad goes, and he gets attacked by wolves and grr... grr!! They attack! *Arrrarr rar... grrr!!* ...and then he gets thrown into the dungeon, and Beast says Belle can stay instead and she does it.

(For the record honey, that's total bullshit, someone ever has me, and they say they'd take you instead, I want you to kick 'em in the balls and run the other way, okay?)

So she stays and then there's singing flatware and she and Beast have some kinda fight and she totally overreacts runs off in a huff and then Beast goes after her... and the wolves attack!! *Grrr... arrrararrr...!!* Beast fights 'em off one-handed!! *Arrraarrr!!!*

Okay, so they make up and then Belle's dad goes into town and starts telling some crap about singing flatware and beasts and they throw him into jail for that little LSD problem and then they take off on Beast and he and Gaston... *arrr! grrr!!* Fight! And Gaston STABS HIM! And she cries!! And she thinks Beast is dead but he's totally not, Gaston falls to his death in a broken mess at the bottom of the ravine, 'cause Beast's not messing around, you cross a guy, stab him in the back, you're going to start some shit and Beast finished it. The end."

posted by Elizabeth at 8:48 a.m.

A Woman on the Edge

Friday, January 14, 2005

Karin: I finally figured out what to do with my widow's peak. This gray streak down the middle makes me look a gazillion years older but it's expensive to dye it and I don't want to mess with the home kits so... I bought some Grecian 5 man formula.

Me: Grecian 5?

Karin: It's for beards. It was like five bucks. I can paint it on while the kids are in the tub. It's hair dye, should work, right?

Me: Oh, swell, cost and time efficient. My favorites.

Karin: Speaking of hair... what's the plan for Mary?

Me: Why, you think I need one?

(Mare trying desperately to see her Little People gym set under a cascade of unkempt hair.)

Karin: Oh. Well... does she let you put barrettes and stuff in it?

Me: Who has time to be batted about the head and shoulders by a toddler? Too much to do in the morning as it is.

Karin: Right. Of course. (long pause.) You know you could cut bangs.

Me: Honestly, K, I don't think you're in any position to advise me on hair. I can't help but notice your kid's Barbie's had a little accident.

K: Oh, that. Her hair was all uneven. So I gave her a bob. At first I was just going to even it out because it made me crazy that her hair was all uneven, you know? Just looking at it day after day made me nuts.

Me: She looks like she woke up drunk on a bathroom floor after a smackdown.

K: Yeah. Once I started, I couldn't stop. Honestly, E, I think I'm on the edge.

Me: I totally think so.

posted by Elizabeth at 5:41 p.m.

MUSH, TUSH, CAT & HORSIE

Sunday, January 16, 2005

All these freaking stuffed animals.

I don't know how they got here. I've never purchased a stuffed animal for this child, and yet we've got enough to stock the ark and a good-sized barn.

After years of disinterest, Mary has finally noticed them. We went from stack of unnamed fuzz to Tush the Bear, Mush the Other Bear, Cat the Third Bear and Horsie the Horse. Tucking Mary into bed at night is a study of toddler politics. Recently, Mush, who had long been assured of the spot under Mary's arm, was moved to the outside after he made the disappointing choice to allow himself to be hauled away by the dog earlier in the day. My heart went out to the poor thing that night, fur matted with dog slobber, consigned to sleeping by Tush the Bear.

Mary did, however, still insist that I tuck Mush in and kiss him.

Horsie the Horse is the current king of the heap. He follows Mary loyally around, being dragged by one poor hoof while the rest of him sweeps up dog hair, cat hair and stray toddler snacks off my floor. (I'm totally going to hook a Swiffer pad up to him.)

Last night as Mary was getting ready for bed, she noticed Horsie the Horse was missing. Daddy was charged with locating him while I got Mary and the rest of the gang tucked in.

Daddy appeared at the foot of the bed looking, well... scared.

"Okay, Mare, here's the deal," he said. "Horsie... is out on an adventure. He left a message with his secretary to let you know that he's out with Chloe the dragon, that they're fine, and they hope to see you soon."

Blink, blink.

"So... he said to go ahead without him. And he'll check in in the morning. 'Kay?"

Blink, blink.

"Horsie, pwease."

"No, see, honey, Chloe and Horsie, well, okay. See, Shrek called and asked for them. Horsie won't be gone long – "

"Shrek needs Horsie?"

"YES!! Exactly! So you understand, it'll be a while."

"Okay. Daddy." Blink, blink. "Horsie, pwease?"

It's so sad to see a grown man at the mercy of a two year old.

"Look, Baby, Horsie... I didn't want to tell you this but Horsie forgot to file form 3316 A of the Internal Revenue code and now they've got him in a dark room and it's going to be at least a week before they have enough answers, okay? Horsie's fried. Horsie thought he could beat the system and now Horsie got f – "

"Momma's gonna go look for Horsie, honey. Wait here with Daddy."

I am happy to report that it's true, once you are a mother your Finding Things gene kicks in – Horsie was not actually locked into a room with angry IRS agents. He was on the living room floor. Covered in dog slobber.

"DAMN IT HORSIE," I whispered. "You want to ruin everything? – if you're not careful she'll have you sleeping in the hamper with Creepy the Mouse who just couldn't wipe that smug look off his face. STRAIGHTEN UP!"

I brushed off the slobber and Mary let him in beside her and Horsie and I kept things between us.

I did get a little sleep this morning, which I appreciated. But you know how you start to wake up and you start registering things that had been going on around you for quite a while?

Actually, it was the camera flash that got me. That's just never a good sign when one is sleeping.

Please note the Clara ornament in my hand and the wreath of flowers in my hair.

posted by Elizabeth at 2:01 a.m.

Up Crib...Down, Homer!

Tuesday, January 18, 2005

Mary has learned to climb out of her crib.

I made this discovery last week. I had put Mary down for a nap and was in the next room on a phone call. After I hung up the phone there was a very polite knock on the bedroom door.

I opened it, and there she stood.

"No nap, thanks," she said.

I looked over and her crib was buttoned up, just exactly as I had left it.

"Mare... how'd you get out of your crib, honey?"

"Up crib. Down dresser."

Do it once it's a fluke: explain how you did it and it's time for a bed.

So we whisked the crib away and Mary was shortly in possession of a brand new toddler bed. Pink, of course. With cute pink sheets and pink fleecy blanket.

You totally know where this is going.

So we're on our second week of Sleeping With Momma When We Sleep At All. Naptime is actually exercise time: put Mary down, give hugs and kisses, and then go out and wait for her to come out and need to be escorted back to bed. Our record was nine times in one hour.

Night time is even worse.

"Back to bed please, Mary. You had your story and your song and your water. Time to sleep."

"Momma cuddle?"

Awe, c'mon. That's dirty pool. Come on.

So it is that after three hours of "back to bed, please" I collapse into bed beside my toddler for my few hours of kick-punctuated rest.

I'm sleep-deprived folks. I'm strung out and some sort of major mental collapse is imminent.

Mary had hers last night.

I was working at the computer when I heard Mary let out a bloodcurdling shriek. After counting limbs and eyeballs I asked her what on Earth was wrong. That was when I learned that a giant purple fish named Homer had invaded my bed and frightened my child and was, even as as I stood there, staring at her menacingly. I couldn't see him of course, but any time she looked over her shoulder he was there and she shrieked and clung to me shouting, "SCAWED!"

So of course I got in beside her. This was not quite enough security for Mary who proceeded to roll on top of me and burrow her head under the blankets shouting, "GO AWAY HOMER!"

Homer?! "Mare, do you think Momma's afraid of Homer?"

Long pause, and a very small, "Yes."

"No, baby, Momma's not afraid of Homer. The only thing that ever scares Momma is when Mary isn't safe. Mary running away in a store scares Momma. Not holding hands in parking lots scares Momma. But Homer... Homer's just a punk."

So the hours passed. She would drift into sleep and then the wind would blow and she would start awake, saying, "Whas'at?"

"It was the wind."

"It was *Homer*!"

"Momma's not scared of Homer, baby, Momma's not... zzzzz."

"HOMER'S SCAWEY!!!"

"Okay, that's it. Where's Homer? Point to him. Homer. Get over here. I've had enough of this. You're scaring Mary and this is her – er – my bed and I've had it with your heavy breathing and cold stare. You have to do what I say, Homer, because I am Da Momma. Now **get out!!**"

"Momma..." my child said in awe. "Momma... *not scawed*."

That's right, baby. I'm a hero! A very, very sleepy hero.

posted by Elizabeth at 10:32 a.m.

AHHHHH...

Wednesday, January 19, 2005

Whenever we're threatening to be snowed in for a while, I hit Walgreens to see if I can pick up a new toy that's interactive, complex, and oh... *quiet*.

But we'd exhausted the Walgreens inventory last blizzard, so when we were expecting snow two days ago, I was reduced to hitting the fancy-schmancy toy shop in town.

I found a Noah's ark that attaches to the edge of the bathtub. It included a bubble maker, a swimming fish, and a water wheel that looked suspiciously to me like it would be good for squirting the dog if she was bugging ya too much. It was twenty bucks, but what the heck.

Little naked Mary was hanging out all excited to try the dog-spitter but right away there were problems. The toy didn't stick to the edge of the tub very well, which meant I had to hold it which is NOT the purpose of the Blizzard Distraction Toy. (The purpose is for Momma to read a book while Mary entertains herself for a while.)

The bubble blower was only mildly satisfying and took too much effort to fire up. The swimming fish in the middle was constantly running out of water and the push-function that was supposed to make him dance just made him look like he had really bad gas.

Mary was all done with this toy in about three minutes.

Last night, I figured we'd try it one more time. With all the excitement of the night before, a nice long soaky bath before bed would be a good break for us both. While the water steamed, I brought out the Noah's ark and attempted to find the magic trick for attaching it to the tub.

An earsplitting shriek stopped me cold. Mary raised her hand, pointed to the flatulent fish and screamed, "**HOMER!!!!!!!!!!!!!!**"

Ah.

posted by Elizabeth at 9:28 a.m.

THAT LITTLE NERVOUS BREAKDOWN
WE'VE ALL BEEN WAITING FOR
Saturday, January 22, 2005

I admit to getting punchy. It's been a long sleepless couple of weeks and we're expecting more snow. Tons more. A veritable shitload to be precise.

So we were lying in a heap on the bed this morning trying to decide who's going to brave the market to lay in a supply of milk and fruit bar. While we were talking Mary casually and utterly without provocation hauled off and smacked the dog.

Just like that. No reason, no explanation, just smack, yawn, what's for breakfast. Ginny sat there blinking confusedly.

"Mary," Cute Husband said. "Apologize to the dog."

"No," Mary said, matter-of-factly. She wasn't particularly defiant; she just didn't seem to think it was a good idea.

This is where it got bad: I laughed. I laughed until I couldn't breathe, and then I inhaled, wiped tears from my cheeks, and laughed some more.

Cute Husband was livid, which for some reason was even funnier to me.

"I can't believe you're laughing," he said, in a deadly serious tone. "I mean, if she weren't here, I'd be laughing too, but laughing in front of her..."

Do you know, he didn't crack a grin through that entire speech? Of course, I thought that was even richer, and laughed some more.

"Do you know how bad it is that you laughed?" he demanded. Now I was guffawing. *Of course I know, silly, if you were doing this I'd'a smacked you a few cackles ago. This totally undermines our authority which is, of course, what makes it so freaking funny.*

After staring at me dumbly for a few long seconds, Mary finally leaned over, put her face up in mine and shouted, "Noooooooooooooooooooooooo!!!!! MWAHAHAHAHAHAHAHA." And we rolled around laughing some more.

It's now open season on the dog in La Casa Looney Tunes.

posted by Elizabeth at 4:11 p.m.

OVERHEARD AT LA CASA LOONEY TUNES, BLIZZARD(S) OF '05

Thursday, January 27, 2005

"Mary... stop smearing Chapstick on your face please. Liz, why didn't you take the chapstick away from her?"

"I did."

"You didn't – look, over there, she's caking it on her lips. Could you stop her?"

"Why don't you stop her – I stopped her last time so it's your turn."

"You botched the job, so it's really still your turn."

"I'm telling you I took the Chapstick away – oh. That's a glue stick. Your turn."

"It's freaking cold."

"It is."

"It's really damned freaking cold."

"It really damned is."

"If it gets any colder, I'm gonna open up the dog and crawl inside her like Han Solo in Empire Strikes Back."

"That was Luke Skywalker."

"Oh, yeah. I hate him."

"I don't know how the Eskimos stand it. Really, I don't."

"They eat moldy seal flippers."

"See, we should be grateful. At least we have electricity. If we had a hankering for seal flippers, ours would be fresh."

"Honestly, the Eskimos have no excuse either, with all that freaking snow."

"Mary, please stop smearing glue stick all over your face. We mean it this time."

"If we watch *Mary Poppins* one more time I'm killing the dog."

"Abusing that poor animal is a real theme with you."

"I'm just saying is all."

"I think the dog has to pee."

"So let her out."

"Really? – c'mon, it's cold."

"Sheesh. One minute you want to slice and dice her but when it comes to a little chill you're ready to let her pee inside? She's a dog. Out she goes."

(Comes back later.)

"You know. I'm glad you made me do that. I would have been sorry if I'd lived my whole life without seeing dog pee spatter across our porch in 60 mile-an-hour winds. The best part is how fast it froze. Really, I'm sorry you missed it. Next time you be sure to take her out, okay?"

posted by Elizabeth at 1:35 p.m.

Um, I Dunno Where She Gets That
Saturday, January 29, 2005

Our neighbor's dog, Conrad, loves to come up to our porch, root through our garbage, torture our dog and set off a barking episode that lasts much of the afternoon.

Conrad is not our friend.

But the neighbors are, so instead of yelling at them, we yell at their dog really loudly in the hopes they'll hear us and take the hint. So far, not much luck.

And then one fine day we were driving down the road, and I saw our neighbors walking Conrad. I had just rolled the window down to say hello when Mary's face lit up with recognition and she shouted, "CONRAD GO HOME!!" at the top of her lungs.

You'd think I'd be embarrassed, but actually, I'm relieved she chose to copy me.

She could have copied Daddy, and "Shut up, fuckball," just wouldn't be attractive on a two year old.

posted by Elizabeth at 6:21 p.m.

TUTUS, BOOGERS & QUESADILLAS...
A DAY IN THE LIFE
Sunday, January 30, 2005

I love the pre-child couples. You can spot 'em a mile away, holding hands, no stains on their clothing, admiring your little one with smiles that say, "Some day, *that will be us.*"

So cute. So easily frightened.

Today I took Mary to Baja Fresh. The chain's use of the word "FRESH FRESH FRESH!!" next to all of its menu items makes me twitch, but I thought Mary might be in to it.

I kind of forget that most people don't wear tutus with their winter outerwear, I'm so used to seeing it.

"Look at her, what an angel!" people kept whispering. I puffed up with pride for a second before I realized it is not Mary's manners that caught their attention, but the layers of tulle emanating from her midsection. It goes well with the pink parka and the pink boots.

The most precious hand-holding couple in all the world was smiling at us while I got Mare situated in a booth. Their grins became positively doting as she poured herself a water and smoothed her napkin over her tutu, swinging her feet, waiting for me to bring her quesadilla.

They just about keeled over from Cute when she dipped her quesadilla in salsa took a bite and said, "Yummy Momma! How's yours?"

But it was when she opened her maw and dropped a mucus-covered mudslide of runny cheese and beans down the front of my sweater we really had their attention.

"Yucky, no likeit," Mary said, shaking her head soberly.

"'Sokay, babe," I said. "Try some rice. Don't pick your nose, please."

"Momma, eat'n a booger!!"

"I'd really rather you didn't."

"YUM!"

"'Kay, all done, now let's have some rice."

The couple was frozen in horror.

"I used to write legislation," I informed them as I dabbed at my sweater with a wet napkin. "My words are entered into the Congressional Record."

They laughed nervously.

I bet they talked the whole way home about how their children won't eat boogers and spit food at their parents.

posted by Elizabeth at 9:23 p.m.

DaMomma Sleeps

Friday, February 04, 2005

Mare's having sleep issues. Which means I am having sleep issues.

Cute Husband decided to be my hero and get up with Mary and even handle some chores while I slept in.

He decided to mop the floors and left Mary in the den with *Sesame Street* on and the admonition to, "Stay here. Do not go see Momma. Momma is sleeping."

Fifteen seconds later a pair of blue eyes peered over the mattress at me.

"Momma? You sleep'n?"

"Yes. Sweet lamb. I'm sleeping."

"Wanna cuddle?"

"Sure. I'd love to cuddle." Somehow I hauled all thirty pounds of her over the side and brought her in with me. I smelled her hair and closed my eyes and sank into a deep soft sleep.

"Momma!" she said in a voice that couldn't have been as loud as it seemed. "MOMMA! Wead?"

"Um. No. Sweetie. I don't want to read I want to sleep."

"'Kay."

I heard a page turn.

"'Night moon. 'Night stars. 'Night cow jumping over da moon ... 'night mush. 'Night ol' lady whispering" (here, a dramatic pause) "Husssssh!"

"MARY." From the door way, Cute Husband loomed. "I told you to leave Momma alone."

"Weading."

"Right. Please go wait in the den so Momma can sleep and Daddy can finish chores and we can go?"

"'Night, Momma!"

Once again, I sank, breathing deeply.

"Momma?"

"Hello, sweetheart. I bet your Daddy is off doing something?"

"Yes. Trash."

"Right."

"Momma?"

"Mare, Momma is really tired. Really, really, really, really tired. Momma is going to be very grumpy if I don't get some sleep."

"Gwumpy? Sad? Momma cry?"

"YES! That's it exactly! Momma will CRY if I don't get some sleep pretty damned soon."

She turned on her heels and marched off, and I thought we had it, I found the perfect spot among the pillows, lay back, sighed deeply and started to drift...

"Liz, are you okay?" Cute Husband rushed into the room. "Mary said you were sad and crying and needed help."

"Please go away," I cried. "Please, I just want to sleep."

"Okay, sorry, hon, we're outta here, we're going to the dump, you sleep, okay?"

The door shut, I heard the car rumble away and I almost cried for joy. Now, at last...

"Arroooooooo!" a hopeless, pitiful sound with all the melody of a rusty can opener.

"You need to go out Ginny, don't you?"

"Aroo."

"Right."

HARRY AND THE JOHN
Tuesday, February 08, 2005

Tragedy has struck.

Harry IV is dead.

Of course, we knew it was coming.

Harry – all of them – was a very small but personable goldfish. Harry the First arrived one weekend last summer when Ellie was away and Dad Steve was desperate for something – anything – to make the time go faster. So it was that Ellie came home to one more mouth to feed – or overfeed as the case may be. Harry II was tickled to death. We're not exactly sure what befell Harry III, only that it was fast and deadly and his stare never was quite right.

Ellie really thought she had it this time. Harry IV was fed – like the rest of the family – on a schedule. No tickling was permitted. And she even bought him some lovely plastic greenery to keep him from getting bored.

And yet somehow a few mornings ago when Greta came in to say good morning to Mr. Harry he was floating, bug eyed, at the top of his little bowl.

Greta's too old to buy the "sleeping" bit. Too savvy for the bait and switch. She had to be told the truth.

"Harry is going to visit Nemo," Ellie said as she stood poised with the corpse over the john. "This is the best way to get to him. Say bye-bye Harry! Say hi to Nemo for us!" And with that, she sent Harry to his glory.

Greta seemed nonplussed by these events when she introduced us to her new pet fish, Fifi. ("Seemed more fortuitous than 'Harry,'" Ellie says. Good call.) Fifi was wildly adored for a few milliseconds before the girls were on to other things. They played for a bit, and then marked their path on the way to becoming teenagers by shutting themselves into the bathroom and giggling furiously.

I peeked in on them to see what all the giggling was about and was a little taken aback: two toddlers, standing over an open toilet, were taking turns hocking loogies and giggling.

"Oh," Ellie said from the doorway. "Sorry. Steve, you know, had a hard cold. Phlegm. You know."

"Right. And this is the reason my child can now out-spit most of the major league ball players in America?"

"Yeah. Okay, girls, c'mon time for snacks – what the...?"

Oh dear. There was definitely something wrong with that toilet. As in: don't-flush-call-a-plumber wrong.

While the girls sat eating their snacks Ellie leveled the full focus of her maternal instinct on her daughter.

"Greta. Remember that bologna sandwich? The one you ate really fast today?"

"Yeah?"

"The one that I thought maybe you fed to the dog, it disappeared so fast?"

"Yeah."

"Did you feed it to the dog?"

"No."

"Right. You said that the first time. I'm sorry for not believing you. Did you flush it down the toilet?"

"Yeah."

You know, of course, the problem.

Harry was hungry.

SOME DAYS YOU AIN'T
Wednesday, February 16, 2005

"Mare, you can have the milk in the big cup if you don't spill, okay?"

"Okay, Momma."

Two seconds later the unmistakable sound of milk cascading onto a hardwood floor. I look over and the little rat has done it on purpose, her eyes gleaming with joy.

I picked her up and plopped her into a chair in the corner, so furious I could hardly breathe.

"You stay here for two minutes for spilling the milk on purpose."

She sat in that chair and laughed at me. Hahahahahahaha-freaking-ha.

This was Mary's first-ever time out and so far she seemed pretty unimpressed.

I marched over, sat down and looked her in the eye and said, "Mary, you had to sit here because you deliberately spilled milk. Can you please apologize to Momma; say you're sorry for spilling milk?"

"No." Blink, blink.

Oh. Huh. Well.

"Mary. Momma needs you to say you're sorry for spilling milk on the floor. It is wasteful, it is rude, it is messy. Please say you're sorry."

"Um. No."

 I'm Maverick in *Top Gun*: Moment of choice – do you turn and immediately go to guns? Do you hit the brakes and he'll slide right by?

"Okay, so you're not sorry," I said. "Fine. Great. Doesn't bother me a bit. If you spill milk again, Mary, you're going back to the chair, okay?"

(Obligingly) "Okay, Momma."

Some days you're hot. Some days you just ain't.

posted by Elizabeth at 11:03 p.m.

HOUIE'S ON THE LAM

Thursday, February 17, 2005

Last night Mary left the front door open just long enough for our two cats to escape. I recovered Pedro fairly quickly, but my last glimpse of Houie was of his abnormally large feline posterior jumping excitedly over the porch and diving under the house.

The last time this happened, Cute Husband got cammied up in his old Marine Corps uniform to belly crawl under the porch. He was covered in mud, cat spit and scratches, but he brought Houie out.

So he thought he knew the drill when he got cammied up this morning to crawl under the house. Unfortunately, the little bastard has quite a learning curve. He was long gone by the time Cute Husband got under there. Kind of embarrassing when a thirty pound cat can stay ahead of some of the best special operations training in the world.

Really. You, the taxpayer, ought to know.

So Cute Husband did a foot patrol around the perimeter of the house and caught a glimpse of the cat darting into a basement crawlspace. With a sense of purpose bolstered by 200 years of Corps pride, he dove in after him, crawling his way to the furnace and glory.

Houie - while in cat terms roughly the size of Liza Minnelli and Liz Taylor strapped together around a rack of lamb - is a nimble little thing. He shimmed up into some insulation and disappeared like the morning mist.

Cute Husband swears he's got him pinned now. He's blocked the crawlspace and locked down the basement and he tells me I can count on Houie's resolve breaking sometime very soon.

I've been down to the basement a couple of times since and no sign of him. This means either that Houie is not trapped in the basement, or that he is laughing too hard to hear us calling him.

I'll keep you updated.

posted by Elizabeth at 10:19 a.m.

OH, DEAR – HE'S GOING "TACTICAL"

Thursday, February 17, 2005

We have an update.

He grumbled a bit about my blog ("I'd like to see you climb up into that hellhole crawlspace in your pink pajamas... make fun of my cammies... damned civilians...") and then shut himself into a room.

He emerged wearing goggles, industrial gloves, and a face mask.

"You know every time I've had to rescue that cat, he's gone for the eyes," he said. "Now I'm going to crawl up inside the house, and I'm gonna get him and he's not gonna scratch me... do you have a small leash or something?"

"A leash? For Houie?"

"Yeah. I don't expect him to walk on it or anything. You know, just to strangle him a bit, so I can –"

"Strangle him?"

"Well, no not strangle, exactly..." Of course not. That would be wrong.

I handed him a pillowcase and told him to throw Houie in it. His shoulders slumped just a fraction, but he resolutely lowered his goggles, grabbed his Maglite, and headed for the crawlspace.

Semper fi, my friend.

posted by Elizabeth at 12:10 p.m.

HMMM...

He crawled. He looked. He pulled stuff down and moved stuff over.

No sign of Houie.

He's drinking a beer and contemplating his next move.

posted by Elizabeth at 1:59 p.m.

Apprehended
Friday, February 18, 2005

When I found Houie abandoned in a dumpster outside Houston Texas in 1997 he scratched me so badly I almost had to go the ER.

When he escaped in North Carolina in 2000 he engaged a neighboring cat in a fight so severe the other cat never walked the same again. Houie was unscathed.

When he escaped in Boston in 2004, it took two adults two hours to wrestle him from under a tiny filthy porch.

So tonight's capture was maybe a little anti-climactic.

I must emphasize that it was the sealing of the basement that made the apprehension possible.

Sometime after dinner I went into the basement with a Maglite, trained it into a few corners and found Houie wedged tightly into one of them. I sat down, poured some water into a dish, and coaxed him out. He climbed willingly into my arms and home we went.

Houie is safe and sound, and relatively undisturbed except for Cute Husband, who keeps shining the MagLite in his eyes and shouting, "REMEMBER ME FUCKBALL???"

posted by Elizabeth at 7:53 p.m.

FEVERISH
Monday, February 21, 2005

Mare was running a high fever this weekend for only the second time in her life. Cute Husband asked if we had a thermometer, and the truth is, I have no idea where. We moved since her last fever.

Besides, I don't think the degrees themselves matter so much.

For example, Mary woke up at 3 a.m. Sunday going "Momma! Danc'n kitties! I wanna dance with the kitties!" Not a cat in sight.

See, think of the four bucks I saved myself. Imagine how silly I would have felt if I'd been tracking her temperature faithfully all night only to have it be so flipping obvious when it got high enough to power a small New England town?

posted by Elizabeth at 8:15 p.m.

Man, She's GOOOOD

Thursday, February 24, 2005

Pardon me while I feel very sorry for myself. Cute Husband is on Spring Break and he took Mare to the art museum today. They were gone all day while I stayed home puking and watching really bad daytime television.

Have I mentioned we don't have cable?

Oh the woe.

I learned that Jerry Springer is still on the air. That chick from All My Children who was my age now has a boy old enough to speak lines in dramatic scenes. That can't be right. If you're careful with the clicker you can actually watch reality court shows for the better part of three hours, uninterrupted. Channel 18 runs Cagney and Lacy re-runs. Oh my goodness the eighties were a goofy time.

Mare came home and bounded up the stairs to tell me all about her day.

Being her mother, my very first question was, "What did you have for lunch?"

Without hesitating, she said, "Chips and chockit cake!!"

I raised one eyebrow in the general direction of the husband.

"It was like this, see..." he began.

Today, Mary is feeling:

FREE!!

posted by Elizabeth at 6:38 p.m.

MINI-ME
Wednesday, March 02, 2005

Suddenly, your child is talking. And suddenly, you hear how you sound sometimes.

Mary was pretending to wash my face. She paused, clasped my chin in her hands, peered in at me and said in a tone of wonder, "Momma... *you're getting so big!*"

Later I was enjoying a moment's peace after finally getting Mary down for her nap. There was a polite knock at the office door and there she stood. She stretched and said, "Ahhh... *good nap*, Momma! Time to play!" For two hours yesterday I would put her down, go back to the office, and a few minutes later she'd be standing there saying, "GOOD NAP, MOMMA!"

She was getting herself ready for school when I heard her shrieking, "MOMMA IT'S TURKEY!! IT'S TURKEY!"

I came running to find her trying to get her lace-up shoes on by herself. "Oh yes, baby, that is *tricky.*"

When I collected Mare from a play date at El's house she had a bruise on her forehead. I asked her about it and she matter-of-factly said, "Fell off the couch. Hit the floor. Missed the coffee table, *woo hoo!!*"

posted by Elizabeth at 9:27 a.m.

The Toughest Job You'll Ever Love

Wednesday, March 09, 2005

Get a bunch of Marines in a room together and it won't be long before they start telling OCS* or Parris Island stories. These are their stories of boot camp, of their initiation into the Brother-and-Sisterhood, of what it was to go in one person, be broken down, and come out another.

All the listening Marines will guffaw at each other's most defeating, most humiliating moments.

"Oh man, I remember the time I'd been up for two days straight, half dead, covered in mud and slime, and hehehe... I'm dragging myself through the mud and Sergeant Instructor says to me, ' you're only going to fail tomorrow, why don't you just give up and go home now?' Woo hoo! Worst moment of my whole life! Man that was funny!" And everyone in the room does think that's funny.

Sounds pretty barbaric until you get a bunch of moms together over coffee and realize the conversation is pretty much the same. "So there I was in screaming agony, thinking, 'I don't want this baby that badly,' and the doctor says, 'Guess what, it's time to push!' and I started bawling hysterically. Man that was funny!"

Motherhood is war. It's a campaign against your own fears, against the staggering odds of egg meeting sperm and creating a human being; it's armed battle against illness, child predators, bad nutrition and the lure of sugary soda. It's the knock-down-drag-out fight to get your kid across the finish line in one piece – and the realization that there is no finish line. That for the rest of your life you'll worry about your child, and then your child's children. You will never again care about yourself quite so much as you did before.

Cute Husband and I are at the starting line again. If all goes well, Mary will be a big sister in late September. It's thrilling and it's terrifying.

I suffer from severe morning sickness ("hyperemesis gravidarum" – doesn't that make it sound noble??) It has had me out of commission for most of the last six weeks. I'm down fifteen pounds and dragging myself through the days with lots of help from friends. I was this sick with Mary, and it has been a revelation. I suffered this much, and yet somehow I forgot. I am sure I'll forget with this one too.

Some day. Maybe.

*Officers' Candidate School

This morning we're having our gazillionth blizzard in the Boston area. I looked out the window at the lovely icy world blanketed in soft billowy snow and promptly burst into tears.

"WHAT THE HELL DAY IS THIS MARCH 7TH OR SOMETHING??? WHO DID WE PISS OFF????" But I was talking to myself. Cute Husband was at school, it was 6:30 in the morning and my kid needed breakfast, barfing or no barfing.

I managed through getting her some breakfast, ("We can make popcorn for special treat!" I promised her) threw up, and crawled tearfully back into bed. Snow meant no school, it meant no play date this afternoon, it meant me and Mary and no help all day.

"It'll all be okay," I muttered desperately into my pillow. The phone rang. Miss Caitlin was calling to tell us school was on.

WOO. HOO.

I got the kid dressed and then she started to sob. She wanted popcorn. (Rookie mistake: you never offer a toddler something you don't plan to deliver on right this second.) So we quickly made some and put it in a bag for her school friends. We were out the door just three minutes late.

The driver's side of the car had iced over so badly that none of the doors would open. I slipped around, toddler in arms, to the other side, hauled back on the door and it popped open. I got her into the seat and then dragged myself over the gear shift and into the driver's seat. Despite her 200,000 miles Nattie purred right to life. God bless Nissan.

The ice was so thick on the driver's side, I couldn't make much headway with the scraper, so couldn't see much. I made my way down the snowy roads trying to avoid left turns at all costs. We were almost to school when Mary, in a spectacular display, ralphed all over herself. She has barfed less than half a dozen times in her life and most of them were in the most impossible-to-wash car seat ever invented.

I pulled into someone's snowy driveway, threw all my weight against my door and got it open. I got Mary's door open and stood there for one long second. She was strapped into her seat, covered in very yucky stuff, weeping sorrowfully.

This was a freaking nightmare.

I wiped her face and cooed lovingly at her, pausing long enough to throw up myself. I gave her the bad news that we were back to Plan A - no school - and her weeping grew in volume and sorrow. I promised we would bring popcorn to school next time, cooed some more and got back behind the wheel.

Wouldn't you know it? Now my door wouldn't close. So it was that I drove us home through the snow, shifting with one hand, holding the door shut with another, steering with a spare hand I picked up somewhere along the way, fighting gags, reassuring Mary that we'd have a lovely day anyway.

This is motherhood. This is war. Someday this will be very funny.

I gagged my way through peeling off her layers (man she got some coverage – even her socks!) and then took her up to the office. She's sitting in front of the *Sound of Music* eating popcorn and muttering to herself. I have eleven hours until bedtime.

For now, though, I'm just waiting to see what popcorn puke looks like. I promise to share when I find out.

posted by Elizabeth at 9:11 a.m.

I WAS SO WRONG, SO VERY, VERY WRONG

Puke is not the worst. Not by a long shot.

This day will never end.

posted by Elizabeth at 11:28 a.m.

TURNS OUT THIS FAT LADY WAS A CANINE
Wednesday, March 09, 2005

I did it. She's in bed. I got through it. I don't know how, but somehow, we made it, the kid and I.

Under normal conditions, it would be time for a martini. However, that being out of the question, I settled for a bowl of very cold cut fruit, the one thing that appeals.

I sat down and let out a deep sigh.

That was when the dog came up, hacked twice, and barfed at my feet.

I shit you not.

And, of course, it set me right off. She barfed. I barfed.

And with that my friends, I bid you good night.

posted by Elizabeth at 9:44 p.m.

Fun with Barf:
A Hyperemesis Gravidarum Q&A

Thursday, March 10, 2005

What is hyperemesis gravidarum?
It's Latin for "Barfing a Whole Lot While Pregnant."

How does it feel to have hyperemesis gravidarum?
Okay, imagine the worst flu you've ever had. Imagine it continues without relief for weeks or months. Now imagine some nice stranger suggesting that if you sniff ginger and eat saltines you'll feel all better. That's hyperemesis gravidarum.

Who gets it?
Mostly women who did something bad in a former life who God wants to punish. Hahaha just kidding. About two percent of pregnancies are affected by hyperemesis, which has a fancy scientific definition that includes how many pounds you need to lose before anyone takes you seriously. My definition is more simple: If you've ever wrapped yourself around a toilet and begged for someone to hit you with a blunt object and put you out of your misery than either you're really drunk or you have hyperemesis. Your odds of hyperemesis gravidarum improve if you are female.

Have you tried sniffing ginger?
Actually, the one thing I haven't tried is smoking crack. Give me time.

As to the ginger, it made me barf.

Have you tried peppermint?
See ginger.

Does *anything* work?
Well, like I said, I haven't tried the crack yet. But, interestingly, many of the proffered remedies seem to have a similar effect on me. Phenergan, for example, elevates my state of being to the level that I giggle for a bit and pass out. Good news is that I don't barf.

I am currently on Zofran, a relatively new remedy for morning sickness that does take the edge off. It's kept me out of the hospital, which is great, and I only barf once or twice a day now, which is a huge morale boost, lemme tell you. The bad news is that that those tiny little Mother's Helpers cost $20 a pop. That's per pill. I take at least two a day. Our insurance company just denied our last claim. I'm not sure what I'm going to do about that. If I think about it too much, I barf, so let's change topics, huh?

Does Zofran have any side effects?
Giiiiirl I am so not talking about that here. But suffice to say I've done some calculations and I expect my next normal BM to occur sometime around October 7th. (Remember: YOU ASKED!)

This really is a lot of barfing. Have you kept any records of your barfs? Any anecdotes?
I'm so glad you asked. Let's see, the most humiliating barf was when I was about six months along with Mary and I puked in the Baptist Church parking lot of our tiny rural North Carolina town. Yes it was Sunday, and yes people were filing out of services. Matters were not improved by the Marine whacking my back and saying, "WOW that was a good one, good job honey, woo hoo!!"

My most heroic barf was at the end of my pregnancy with Mary when I was eating a delicious croissant in a local bakery, was seized with a familiar rumbling, and flew out the door to toss my cookies in the public trash can on the corner. After I was done I marched back in and finished the croissant.

So far this pregnancy the prize winner was tandem barfing with the dog. Honestly, that was a low moment.

Gee, how do you handle all this big fun?
Quite simply, I've got great friends. El has several times performed door-to-door service, collecting Mare, riding off into the sunset for a few hours, and bringing her back fed and tired.

Karin routinely takes my child into her home and is thoughtful enough to clean her toilet when I come over, in case I need to ralph. We all need such people in our lives. Mare is always returned to me stuffed with treats and wearing little trinkets Emma didn't notice her pilfering from the toy box.

I've also been blessed with great doctors. When all is said and done, it can be hard to love something that is sucking your will to live. Compassionate doctors toss us hyper-emesis girls a few extra sonograms to keep the morale up.

But most important is a great partner. Cute Husband doesn't have time to sleep any more, between law school, shopping for odd cravings, and taking Mare fun places while I barf up all the stuff he worked so hard to buy.

Honestly, you're scaring me. I'm not sure I want children now.
I know. I haven't even told you about labor yet. Don't worry, it'll all be fine. Just remember to sniff ginger. That's key.

posted by Elizabeth at 3:03 p.m.

Big Fun in the ER
Tuesday, March 15, 2005

I spent most of yesterday in the emergency room. Am doing much better today. Got a peek at Little One who sprouted arms and legs since last we looked!

Lots of blog-worthy material, just not much energy. In a couple of days I'll update you on the highlights including:

* Cocaine Boy in the next bed over, and the very patient nurse attempting to get his history even though he kept snoring;

* How Hard it is To Pee When You Have To Carry Your IV Bag Everywhere (and how much you have to pee when you're getting IV fluids);

* Why the "Farr Entrance" is such a freaking clever play on words;

* The lowest moment to date, and why I was bawling on the floor behind the reception desk when it happened.

Stay tuned ...

posted by Elizabeth at 10:27 p.m.

THE STORY BEHIND BIG FUN IN THE ER

Friday, March 18, 2005

If you've ever thrown up a lot – I mean really a lot – to the point that you can't stop, and you're crying, and you feel so horrible you just want to die... then you have some insight to my state of mind in the wee hours of Monday morning. I just wanted something to make the bad man stop.

Around 4:45 we called my mom, woke up Mary, and headed for the hospital.

"Oh, Mare, isn't this fun??" I choked through my gags. "We're going to see Grandma! Special treat! Day with Grandma!"

Long, suspicious look.

"Ice cream?"

"I'm sure Grandma will give you lots of ice cream."

(satisfied) "Okay."

My mom met us at Obstetrics, where they told me they were plum full-up of ladies who actually had babies emerging from their persons that very night. I lay my head down on the table to keep it from moving. (I'm not sure which was moving, table or head, but whatever it was, I needed it to stop.)

My only option, they said, was the emergency room: at a different facility, three blocks away. They were nice enough to hand me a very small, very pink, kidney-shaped basin to barf in on the way.

It was time to let my Mom take Mare so Cute Husband and I could do what we needed to do for Little One and me. We got an elevator and I handed Mary to her Grandma and said goodbye. As the elevator descended, I could hear Mary screaming, "MAAAAAAAAAAAAMMMMMMMMAAAAAAAAAA!!"

That was it for me. I burst into tears. I was too pregnant to take care of my kid, not pregnant enough for the nice people to give me a bed, and all I wanted was to feel normal again.

I cried in the elevator. I cried getting off the elevator. I cried when the nice stranger saw me crying and patted my shoulder. But I reserved my worst sobs for the receptionist who told us there was no shuttle to the Emergency Room, and our best bet was to just walk.

Just then, my Mom came back into the lobby, wrestling a screaming toddler. I dove to the floor behind the receptionists' desk, where I cried and cried some more.

"Ma'am... *are you okay?*" the receptionist leaned down to ask me.

"Shhhh!" I spat, snot and tears running down my face. *"That's my kid!"*

Riiiiight... the receptionist nodded.

"Oh, Mary, look, here, a list of taxis!" My mother said loudly. "We just need to *find a taxi and then we'll go.* But maybe you can help me read this list in case *someone wants to make for the door right now...!*"

Cute Husband grabbed my arm and hauled my heaving, sobbing, gagging self across the lobby, through the doors and out into the early morning.

"No more children," I babbled. "No more."

"I think you said that exactly three years ago," he said, steering me along the sidewalk.

We found the appropriate hospital wing, but when we walked through they told us the Emergency Room was at the other end of it.

I, of course, cried at the news.

"Is she having chest pains or anything?" the woman asked.

Say yes! The little voice inside my head chanted. *They'll bring a stretcher!!*

"No," Cute Husband said.

Traitorous BASTARD!

We went back outside, around the block, where we found the "Farr Entrance." (Farr... hahahaha... get it? Ahahahahahahahaha!!) Would you believe that was still not the freaking Emergency Room?!

We finally found it.

"Please help me," I said to the nice lady behind the counter. "I just want to lie down and barf."

"What's up with this one?" a nurse asked.

"Hyperemesis," the other nurse responded.

"Hyperemesis *gravidarum*," I corrected. The nurse looked startled. "I recently wrote a little question-and-answer essay on it," I informed her.

We filled out our paperwork and were led into the ward to a tiny curtained area with - PRAISE THE LORD - a bed.

My entire plan was to go to sleep and wake up rehydrated and eight months pregnant. This was forestalled initially by Crack Boy in the next bed over, and his very patient nurse.

"Mr. Crack Boy," she was saying. "Can you open your eyes for me, please? Do you know where you are? Mr. Crack Boy, could you please tell me the last time you smoked crack?"

Her interrogatory was met with loud snores.

"Who wants to be in the boring old Maternity Ward, anyway?" Cute Husband asked.

We were attended by The Sweetest Doctor in the World, who hooked me up to some IVs and drugs right quick and was superiorly gifted in the "cooing sympathetically" department. I don't think he came to my bedside once without saying, "Geez, I'm just so sorry you're so sick, it's terrible."

Cute Husband was doing pretty well in the cooing sympathetically department, too. Four bags of fluids will make a girl pee a lot, and the bathroom was a bit of a trek down the hall. He did yeoman's work carrying my IV bag around behind me, and placing himself strategically to cover what my hospital gown did not.

In the end, Dr. Niceguy congratulated me on keeping myself from getting sick enough to stay, and with a *mazel tov* and a glass of juice, told us they needed the bed.

We got home late that night, I barfed once more for old time's sake, and then crawled into bed next to Mary. After six weeks of being pushed off on to other people, hanging out watching videos and watching me throw up, this is the one thing I can still do for her, and she needs it more than ever.

"I'm sorry I'm so sick," I whispered. "But Momma's okay, baby. Momma's okay and it will get better."

"Mary's sad Momma's sick."

"Momma's sad, too," I said. "I wish that I could do more with you. But I will again, soon, I promise." A stab of guilt: bringing a second child into the world had instantaneously made me an inadequate parent to the first. This was followed by another stab of guilt for resenting a tiny little baby who didn't ask to be born.

"Your feet are cold," I said. I put them against my legs and rubbed them. "Is that better, Mare?"

"Yes. Warm. Dank you Momma."

Although it has been going on some time, it still astonishes me that my child can communicate her desires and worries so completely. I was filled with a moment of panic, envisioning myself again with a newborn who knows only stark need.

"I love you, Momma," Mare whispered.

It was the first time she ever said it first.

Mary's firsts are slipping away, and so are mine.

"I love you too, Bug," I whispered back.

Today, Mary is feeling:

posted by Elizabeth at 1:16 p.m.

So This Lawyer Walks into
a Gynecologist's Office...
Wednesday, March 23, 2005

This post deals with early pregnancy and prior pregnancy loss.

The first time we ever had a sonogram was at the end of the first trimester with our first pregnancy. A tiny little baby emerged in the middle of the gray triangle, and we were instantly in love. The doctor gently told us the baby was still and would never move again.

We were never the same.

Ever since then, I have a Pavlov's dog reaction to sonograms. Want to see me pant and shake uncontrollably? Put me on a table with a sonogram screen next to me and a little gray triangle lighting up the darkness.

This pregnancy we have opted for an Early Risk Assessment screening, a sonogram and blood panel combination that checks a first trimester fetus for Trisomy disorders by measuring the thickness of the nuchal fold at the base of the neck. Our office also uses a high-powered sono machine to check for the presence of a nasal bone, which is absent in many Down's babies.

Cute Husband had a conference in Washington this week, so I asked Kara to come with me to the sonogram. We've been friends since we were thirteen. Kara is a Boston lawyer, married to her college sweetheart, and they are the cutest little pre-child couple you've ever seen.

I tried hard not to scare her. Honest.

"Ohmigod are those stirrups??" she hissed while we waited for the blood draw in a small exam room.

"Oh, those are *little* stirrups. You should see the ones in the delivery room!"

She shuddered adorably.

"I don't want to know."

"Oh there're all kinds of stuff no one ever tells you," I chirped helpfully. "You heard about pooping on the delivery table, yet?" Her face blanched.

"Oh, guess not," I said.

The nurse drew blood from my middle finger, wrapping it in a Band-aid.

"Look at my finger!" I said to Kara, shooting her the bird. (When you meet as thirteen year olds, you kind of revert to form when you're together.)

"Did they take your blood?" Dr. Fancymachine asked when he entered the room.

"Yes," I said. "I'd show it to you, but it's rude. Hey Kara... LOOK AT MY FINGER!!" Gosh that just never got old.

And then it was time. I lay back on the table and Dr. Fancymachine squeezed a pile of warm gel squiggles onto my tummy. A low hum, a gentle gray light, and my name on the corner of the screen. I gripped Kara's hand and breathed.

"Please have a heartbeat," I whispered frantically. "Please be okay. Please be okay."

He brought the transducer to my tummy and I inhaled sharply.

"Excuse me, doctor," a woman called from the door. "May I borrow you for a minute?" He put the transducer down and disappeared.

"Hmm..." Kara said.

We sat there, not moving, holding hands.

"This is a joke," I said. "I'm on camera."

"How hard can this thing be to operate?" Kara eyed the keyboard.

"Oh that's not a good idea," I said, with a sudden image of adolescent Kara making her famous cheese sauce at her mother's stove - it ended up in a hard solid mass at the bottom of a pan I'm not sure Kara's parents ever really missed. That's what happened to flour and butter in Kara's hands ~ sonogram transducers were bound to be dangerous.

Five long minutes later, Dr. Fancymachine was back. He plunged the transducer into the pile of gel, and an image came on the screen. I braved a look through squinted eyes.

Little One was moving. Arms and legs were wiggling. I squeezed Kara's hand while Dr. Fancymachine looked, measured, and clucked to himself. He zeroed in on Little One's face with its hollowed eyes and shadowy lips. He froze the screen and made a notation.

"Elizabeth," he said, "baby has a nose."

"I know," I bawled. "I can see it." *Prof. Kypros Nicolaides of London's Harris Birthright Research Centre for Fetal Medicine, checked if 701 unborn babies between the ages of 11 and 14 weeks had a nasal bone. Of the 59 babies later found to have Down's syndrome, 73% did not have a nasal bone.*

I'm down to 27% on that nose.

"C'mon, baby, turn over," he was saying. "C'mon, I just need the right angle on the neck, c'mon..."

C'mon, baby, do it for Mommy. Please honey, please turn.

He got the shot, pressed some buttons and smiled at me.

"That's exactly what we want to see," he said.

"Yeah?" I squeaked. "Really? We're okay?" Next to me, another squeak.

"Oh Kara," I laughed. Her face was wet with tears.

"Yeah," he said. "Everything looks just great. *Textbook.*" Kara squeaked again and the doctor handed us both tissues.

He typed a few words and printed a picture: Little One with an arm raised. "Hi, Mommy!" the caption read. Dr. Fancymachine typed again and another picture printed. "Hi, Kara!" this one said.

Kara's staccato squeaks were punctuated with snorts.

"I was going to wait for the right moment," I said. "We were wondering if you would be our baby's godmother?" Squeak after pitiful squeak with a yes in there somewhere.

We hugged each other, we hugged the doctor, we looked at pictures and cried and hugged some more.

It was late when I got to El's house to collect Mary. She was mad at me for being gone all day, and had three meltdowns between El's house and ours.

The cat had vomited on my pillow. I barfed and changed the sheets.

Finally, I climbed into bed next to Mary, and was asleep before she was. Between us, a small round ball of belly was suddenly obvious to me.

Several hours later, the sound of the front door opening. Cute Husband leaned over me in the darkness, smelling of cold and travel. He kissed my cheek and whispered against my ear, "How's Little One?"

"*Textbook*," I whispered back. "Perfect. Healthy. *Okay.*"

He squeaked, too.

posted by Elizabeth at 1:39 p.m.

I Don't Want to Alarm Anyone, But...

Saturday, March 26, 2005

I seem to have maybe turned some kind of corner here.

We went out to dinner tonight. Like, actually, as a family, all of us, went out to the mall, walked a bit, and then... I got hungry.

So we sat down and our nurse... er... the waitress... described the specials and she was telling us about this mango salmon thing and I interrupted her to say,

"I want that. Oh. And a Caesar salad. Please. Right quick, as quick as you can. Please."

"She's pregnant," my husband whispered to her behind his menu.

One gigantic Caesar salad was plopped down in front of me just seconds later. I ate it. I ate it down to every last delectable green. With it, I ate two of the three dinner rolls on the table. Then I did a bad, bad thing. Mary was coloring, so while she wasn't looking, I ate her clam chowder.

"No Momma!" she said. But it was too late. It was gone. Every drop. I think I licked the bowl.

"Momma ate my chowder!" she protested to her dad.

"You shouldn't leave it so close to her mouth like that," he said.

Then my salmon came, drizzled in mango butter with some kinda something fancy tapenade on the top. There was a pile of broccoli and a baked potato with butter and – Lord save us all – sour cream.

I did toss my kid a few broccoli spears. Is it wrong that I resent her for eating them?

"No dessert?" Cute Husband asked, while I paid the bill.

"Actually, I seem to remember a Godiva store upstairs," I said.

Cute Husband gave up chocolate for Lent. I gave up my figure, alcohol, soft cheese, sushi and feeling well.

I got a chocolate starfish for Mare and a lovely caramel for myself. We held our little gold bags and walked back through Filene's, pausing to admire purses and dresses as we ate our chocolate.

I got her to bed, and as has been my habit lately, was asleep before she was. But I couldn't get it out of my mind. The thought of that luscious salad, all those yummy greens smothered in garlicky yummy...

2:45 a.m..

I've just eaten a grilled cheese, a large bowl of mushroom barley soup and two glasses of milk.

Be afraid. Be very, very afraid.

posted by Elizabeth at 2:46 a.m.

IT'S ALL IN THE TIMING
Tuesday, March 29, 2005

I currently am on three drugs for hyperemesis.

From the insert that came with my Reglan prescription:

"SIDE EFFECTS that may occur while taking this medicine include drowsiness, *restlessness, dizziness, jitteriness, anxiety, agitation, confusing, headache and diarrhea*. CONTACT YOUR DOCTOR IMMEDIATELY if you experience unusual or *uncontrollable movements of arms, legs, face, eyes, tongue, mouth, neck, or jaw*; unusual or unexplained vision changes, fever, sweating; mood changes including depression or *thoughts of hurting yourself*."

From the insert that came with my Zofran:

"SIDE EFFECTS include headache, **constipation**, stomach pain or weakness."

And then the Phenergan:

"Unlikely to occur but report promptly: *restlessness, muscle stiffness, weakness, difficulty speaking, loss of balance, mask- like facial expression, trembling or shaking, dizziness, lip smacking or other uncontrollable movements*, difficulty urinating, skin rash/discoloration."

So, the key as I see it is to take these drugs in the right combination so that:

You stay regular; feel restless and twitchy when there're dishes to be done; and when the suicidal thoughts come you're too drowsy to care.

posted by Elizabeth at 2:48 p.m.

Yeah, But Does She Tell Jokes?

Friday, April 1, 2005

Mare's Gran sent her the most dreamy Easter dress. It's organza, filmy, pink, with pink flowers, and pink trim, and a pink sash.

Mary wears this dress to play with Play-Doh; she wears it to cook pancakes; she wears it to bed. (Let me tell you that co-sleeping next to thirty pounds of squirmy pink organza leads to very bizarre dreams.)

But it's New England, it's March, and I do insist that she wear pants outside. After a week of leaving the dress at home, yesterday Mary solved the problem by wearing pastel striped pants, a royal purple flowered shirt, and over all, the pink organza dress.

"Hm. Clever. Grab your shoes, let's go," I said. We had a slight spat over the pink Mary Janes but I insisted the brown Merrils were more appropriate to the mud.

Never let it be said that I am a pushover.

In the car, she found her Easter bonnet which she promptly screwed onto her head backward so the ribbons were falling jauntily in her eyes. We drove to the market and I put her in a cart, proceeding to the fruit aisle while Mary sang to herself.

"Do! ... a needle pulling thread!" she sang. "La! ... jam and bread!"

"Good singing baby," I muttered, counting out pears.

"Ti... la so... fa me... re do!" she sang, swinging her feet and blowing ribbons out of her eyes.

"That's quite an outfit," some guy standing next to me said. I actually stopped to check what I was wearing.

"Oh, her, right." I studied her carefully while she blinked at me.

"You're right," I said, realizing the problem. "The Mary Janes really would have been better." To her: "I'm sorry Boo."

"LA SO FA ME RE DO!" she said.

posted by Elizabeth at 10:14 p.m.

JUST LIKE MOMMA

Tuesday, April 5, 2005

It is a funny thing, living with a pregnant two-year-old.

Every morning before she gets out of bed, she calls to her daddy to bring, "Cwackers and water, pwease. And for Momma, too."

She sits there beside me in the bed, munching and slurping away and will, occasionally, groan and gag if the mood strikes.

After weeks of scaring her with the mad dashes to the john, I finally decided to include Mare in the fun.

Changing a diaper yesterday morning I felt a familiar rumble.

"Hey, woo-hoo!" I said. "Time to barf, kid, c'mon let's go!!" She grabbed my hand and together we ran to the bathroom. While Mare coughed into the Elmo potty I frantically reached for the lid on the toilet and timed it perfectly ~ lid came up as puke came down and the result was a far-and-wide spatter of lid-catapulted barfum.

Mare laughed and laughed.

Hey we take our amusements where we can find them here at La Casa Looney Tunes.

posted by Elizabeth at 4:03 p.m.

SHE MAY DRESS FUNNY,
BUT SHE GETS PICKED UP ON TIME
Thursday, April 7, 2005

We all have our issues.

One of mine is that I refuse to be late to pick up my kid. Not only is it rude to the person I've left her with; it also makes the kid feel like a burden. When you're the last one picked up all the time, you wonder if there is something about you that is less desirable than the children whose parents were on time.

Cute Husband is studying for finals, which means he's around a lot, but grumpy. He's a bit more available to help out with Mare, though, which I appreciate. Last night we talked about the possibility that he would take Mare to school as usual, only for a break he also would pick her up, give her lunch and put her down for her nap, giving me the better part of the day off.

So when I woke up and there was no note, and Cute Husband's car was gone I was giddy with joy.

Of course, with so much work to do, so many deadlines, I set straight away to checking e-mail and chatting with friends online. I paused to take a picture of my belly for some people who asked for it, and that took a while because as much as I want to be showing, I don't want to look fat, so angles matter.

I had a column due very shortly, but Jib Jab had a new prescription drug cartoon going that was so funny I watched it twice.

Then the phone rang.

"Hi. It's Caitlin."

Caitlin... Caitlin...

"Hi!"

"Um. Hey. Are you coming to get your kid?"

It was 12:20. Pick up time was 11:45.

I didn't stop to change out of my house shorts, didn't stop to run a brush through my hair, but I did stop to drop a tersely worded e-mail to Cute Husband instructing him on the proper use of modern writing utensils. It contained some bad words.

I grabbed the keys and ran and out into the horror of daylight, the warm spring breeze ruffling the hair on my legs. (Note to self: that's icky.)

My kid had watched all her little friends' mothers come and go. I was trying not to picture her standing there bravely; looking up at every opening of the door, hopeful that it was me.

I was gonna kill Cute Husband.

When I got there, Mare was sitting in a circle of three year-olds, rapt as Caitlin read a story to her afternoon crowd. I tiptoed in and did my paperwork, collecting Mary's things.

The story ended and Mare looked up.

"LOOK, MISS CAITLIN!!" she said in breathless reverence. "*It's my Momma!!*"

How much do I suck?

"Sorry," I said sheepishly to Caitlin. She smiled sympathetically. "Was she sad?"

"Do you know what she said when the last kid had gone home?"

"Will you be my Mommy?"

"No. She turned to me and said, 'Miss Caitlin, what's for lunch... peanut butter toast??'"

"She said that?"

"Yeah."

"What did you say?"

"That was when I called you."

She was okay. And then something even better: *She was okay because I've done a good job.*

"Wanna go home, Boo?"

"Yeah, I'm hungry. I want peanut butter toast, milk, grapes, cheese, crackers, milk and peanut butter toast."

"Okay, you can have anything you want, baby." I stopped short of apologizing to her for a lapse she hadn't noticed.

I strapped her in amidst the usual chit chat and updates on Otis the Cat's behavior. We pulled away and I headed for home, short nothing but a deadline. Astonished that it really was okay that I had left her.

We all have our issues. But they don't have to be our kids' issues.

But yes. I was still super-pissed at Cute Husband.

posted by Elizabeth at 12:09 a.m.

TODDLER LOGIC
Monday, April 11, 2005

Every time we go to Whole Foods we stop first at the bell peppers and select one for Mare to chomp while I work the aisles.

Yesterday I had to leave Mary at the checkout for a sec to go back for garlic. This left her in a quandary.

She knew she wasn't allowed to get out of the cart. But she also knew the pepper had to be paid for.

So her next move made perfect sense, but it left the cashier extremely confused as to why a half-eaten bell pepper was hurled at her by a two year old who otherwise looked perfectly non-violent.

The woman Mary hit with the bell pepper is feeling:

SORE

posted by Elizabeth at 2:25 p.m.

Snuffleupagus Could Talk, Too

Thursday, April 19, 2005

In all the months Mary has been visiting Professor Bloom, she has never uttered a word in his presence.

Cute Husband has taken her to school a lot lately because it is so hard for me to take care of her. Professor Bloom is a favorite because whenever she visits he withdraws a treat from an impossible stash of trinkets in his office.

She never talks to him. But she talks about him constantly.

"Pwofesso Bwoom gave me this!" she says, pointing to her new Strawberry Shortcake necklace. "Pwofesso Bwoom gave me an ice cweam twuck!" she says, firing off her new matchbox truck down the edge of the sofa. "Pwofesso Bwoom home with his Mommy, too?" she asks when I put supper before her.

But in front of Professor Bloom, she says absolutely nothing.

Today Cute Husband and Mare brought Professor Bloom a small cheesecake covered in strawberries.

"Thank you, Mary," Professor Bloom said. "I have something for you, too." He handed her a matreshka, a small painted wooden doll he had picked up on a recent trip to Russia. She smiled shyly and whispered her thanks only when prompted.

"Thank you for the cake," he said. "Would you like a strawberry?"

Mare nodded soberly and he handed her the strawberry.

"Really, she talks about you all the time," Cute Husband said. "I swear. She's extremely verbal. Full sentences for some time now."

"Oh, I don't mind," Professor Bloom said. "Bye Mary, enjoy the strawberry!"

"Come on Mary, let's go."

Mary bit into her strawberry as they walked out into the corridor.

"Daddy," she said. "Pwofesso Bwoom is a nice, nice man."

posted by Elizabeth at 10:31 p.m.

It's Nice to Have Friends
Thursday, April 21, 2005

"I don't understand, Karin... I just don't seem to fit in in this town." We were sitting in Karin's living room. Mare and Emma were busy baking muffins at Em's play kitchen.

"I've lived in this town two years and I think until I buy a pair of pink capris and regularly manicure my nails, we'll be short on play dates."

"Yeah, what's up with that? I've had some cold rejections on the playground let me tell you."

"Hey... what happened to your streak?"

"Oh," she said reaching up for the high widow's peak in her short hair. It has gone white again, despite the Grecian 5 applications. "Turns out, men don't routinely shampoo their beards."

"Ahhh... Bummer. So what are you going to do?"

"Buy more Grecian man formula. It's still cheaper."

"Oh good."

"Miss Kawin?" Mare said, tugging on her sleeve.

"Yeah Babe?"

"Tank you for saving my life."

"I'm sorry?" Karin asked.

"It's from *Beauty and the Beast*," I whispered. "She has no idea what it means."

"Oh. You're welcome, Mare. Any time." Mare looked satisfied and went back to cramming her muffin pan at the play oven.

"Maybe if I got a pedicure I'd have more friends," I said.

"Don't spend any money on it. Emma does mine. I'm sure she'd do yours. For a small fee."

"Oh fabulous. I'll have friends in no time."

posted by Elizabeth at 10:06 p.m.

THE HALF-ASSED FLAMMABLE SMURF FREAK

Sunday, April 24, 2005

The following is an actual conversation between me and Cute Husband over Yahoo Instant Messenger today while he studied for finals at the library:

> *Cute Husband:* Ok
> *Cute Husband:* tell you what
> *Cute Husband:* maybe I am working myself too hard.
> *Cute Husband:* I'm going to work for another hour....
> *Cute Husband:* Then home, beer, cards, etc.
> *Cute Husband:* should be there around 6:30
> *Damomma:* Yes yes
> *Damomma:* but first
> *Damomma:* I am dealing with
> *Damomma:* er
> *Damomma:* a bit of a situation here
> *Cute Husband:* what?
>
> *(Cute Husband accepting file transfer request)*

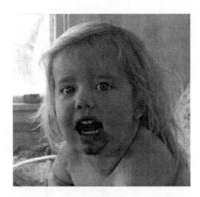

> *Damomma:* And she has a wedgie.
> *Cute Husband:* WTFO?
> *Damomma:* Um.
> *Damomma:* Hello Kitty?
> *Damomma:* Fifteen colors
> *Damomma:* all in one??
> *Damomma:* She
> *Damomma:* um
> *Damomma:* was sucking on it.

Damomma: Saliva+ink

Damomma: = ICK

Damomma: very copious ick.

Cute Husband: She is really screwed

Cute Husband: I still have that damn Hello Kitty ink on me – I COULDN"T WASH IT OFF!!!!

Damomma: OMG

Damomma: I'm putting her in a bath THE PLAY GROUP MOMS WILL NEVER LIKE ME WHEN MY KID LOOKS LIKE A HALF-ASSED SMURF

Cute Husband: USE TURPENTINE

Cute Husband: SHE WILL NEED IT

Damomma: ON HER MOUTH?????

Cute Husband: no

Cute Husband: that doesn't sound right

Damomma: She's singing to herself

Damomma: the cleanup song LIKE THAT FREAKING HELPS YOU BLUE MOUTH FREAK!

Damomma: she's trying to pick up popcorn

Damomma: clean up clean up

Damomma: everybody every where

Damomma: clean up clean up

Cute Husband: See you around 6:30

Cute Husband: GO WITH GOD

Cute Husband has signed out. (4/24/2005 4:23 p.m.)

The following is an actual phone message left on the Voicemail of Damomma's Daddy:

"Hi. It's me. It's about 4:30. And I am wondering if you have any ideas as to how to get permanent ink off of a toddler. No reason. Just … wondering. Let me know if you have any thoughts. Nothing urgent. Just. You know. Lemme know."

The following is an actual voicemail left by Damomma's Daddy:

"Hi, it's your old man. Try lighter fluid or Comet. Although honestly either one could do more harm than good. Good luck."

Great. She's gonna be my little flammable Smurf Freak.

posted by Elizabeth at 8:36 p.m.

CAN SHE BE TRAINED TO WORK THE COFFEE POT?

Monday, May 2, 2005

The hyperemesis is getting better, but now I'm just exhausted all the time.

This morning Cute Husband left the house at o'dark thirty. I vaguely registered the news that he was leaving and that Mare was having her breakfast in the kitchen and I should get up.

"Righargharahamuph..." I think I said.

Later – quite a while later – I woke up under a pile of books and stuffed animals. A pair of gigantic blue eyes was peering in at me, dripping with maternal concern.

"Eat your yogut Momma." A spoon heaped in yogurt was crammed in the general direction of my mouth. I dutifully ate while I contemplated some things.

First, that the yogurt was actually kind of tasty. It was maple.

Second, that I think the yogurt had been in the fridge behind the eggs. How had she gotten to it? And what havoc had she wrecked along the way?

Another spoonful came at me and I moved my mouth to catch it. Sure, yogurt on the sheets was going to be small potatoes to what I suspected waited for me in the kitchen, but best to avoid if possible.

"Milk, Momma?" she asked, proudly producing a sippy. The lid was not on all the way, but it was indeed filled with cold milk.

"Thank you Boo," I said, removing the lid and taking a sip.

"Icy cold," she said. "Yummy."

"Hmm-hmm," I said. "Let's go take a peek at the kitchen, shall we?"

"Momma up?" she asked.

"Oh, either that or this is a protracted nightmare. Let's go see that kitchen."

The eggs were actually fine. The milk was another story. There was a lake of it in the middle of the floor.

"Had some issues with the milk, huh Buggy?"

"Oh," she said in her best soothing voice, "doesn't matter a bit. Be right back." She scampered off and came back with a bath towel fresh from the hamper. She dropped it in the lake and started spreading the milk around the floor. "No pwoblem," she said.

"Right. Momma's gonna have some coffee and a shower, 'kay? You just... keep up the good work."

"Want me to make you some coffee?"

"How about you get your shoes on, we're late for school."

"Okay. Lemme get them out of the dryer."

"Riiiiight."

Today, Mare is feeling:

THOUGHTFUL

posted by Elizabeth at 8:35 p.m.

LOOK, IS IT MY FAULT SHE FORGOT
SHE COULD BARK?

Saturday, May 07, 2005

The hyperemesis is better, but if I'm honest about it, I'm still not doing so hot. I can't do more than one or two things a day and dragging the kid in and out of the car seat exhausts me to the point of tears.

Cute Husband is going into his law finals and he's never home except when he's so tired we're a sick little side show of babbling morons trying to pass a toddler between us.

For the last several weeks, Cute Husband and Aunt Emily have been working to get me to stay with her for a while in New York. The plan would be for her to spend some quality time with Mare while I sleep, eat, and try to get some energy back.

I've resisted. I've actually, really, refused. Most times I'm very excited to go see Emily and her family. But right now I am so tired even thinking about going to New York makes me want to curl into the fetal position and suck my thumb. Sure, what I'm living ain't pretty, but it's working. Sort of. Mostly. Not quite for everyone.

So last night I was very tired. I'd driven to New Hampshire to see a beautiful new baby girl, and I was worn out. I let the dog out and brushed my teeth before staggering to bed.

In the night a cold front came through with a lot of wind and rain. I woke to rain smacking the window and felt sick dread.

"Is everything okay?" I said to Cute Husband. "Is the house leaking? Is Mary okay? I just have this unbelievable panic all of a sudden. Could you check the car and be sure the windows are all up? Oh my God what if the windows are down and I flooded the car??"

"It's only water, honey. Let me go check, okay?"

He opened the door and there on the front porch, huddled under a bench, was one very sad, very wet, very pissed off Basset.

He toweled her off, cooed gently, and brought her a bowl of food while whistling "New York, New York."

"Maybe I can go Monday?" I said the next morning as I watched him pack my suitcase.

"Right... how much underwear you figure on needing? Whatever, here's six pairs."

"Honey... *are you kicking me out?*"

"Yeppers, yes, roger that, that's an affirmative."

So um. I guess Mare and I are off to New York for a bit. Bagel, anyone?

posted by Elizabeth at 3:20 p.m.

DON'T LABOR IN PIGTAILS

Tuesday, May 10, 2005

I was seven months pregnant when the season finale of *Friends* aired and Jennifer Aniston groaned prettily a few times before delivering a baby girl. She looked darling in her pigtails and hospital gown and the word episiotomy was never so much as whispered. Of course her figure was back in no time and her baby wandered in and out of plot lines at the writers' convenience.

This is the birth we're handed in the popular media. It's clean and shiny and pretty, dripping with personal choice, and if we pay too much attention to it, it will do us harm.

My first birth was at 12 weeks gestation. I was heavily sedated, and woke up weeping, my beloved round belly gone. My road to motherhood began there, and ended in another operating room ten months later in a haze of desperate pain.

Mary was handed to me two hours after her birth, a pink-hatted mystery of awe and joy and a little sadness. She possessed me in a way no human being ever had. I had suffered for her and would gladly do it again to keep her safe, and I didn't even know her.

The overwhelming gratitude of her birth in the wake of loss made me a better mother. I am unfazed by the little stuff. Who can mind a smurf-blue toddler as long as she's healthy, alive and free on the Earth?

But lately I've had more bad days than I've wanted to admit. I've gotten through the weeks and months of this pregnancy one foot in front of the other, in a constant state of nausea, guilt and hopefulness. *If I just keep going, it has to get better*, I kept muttering, day after day. But it wasn't getting better. I couldn't gain weight, was barely able to take care of my child, was starting to feel truly broken down. Cute Husband was right – I was so tired I wasn't rational. Just ask the dog.

So finally we went home to my family in New York, Mary was gently taken from me amid her distraught protests while I cried with shame and sorrow and guilty relief that she was suddenly not my problem.

Someone else has been giving my daughter her meals, someone else helped her scale the rock wall at the park. Someone else made the mistake of taking her into a clothing store and was rewarded by two pigtails on either side of an armful of pink outfits, a tiny voice chirping a plaintive, "All mine? Pwease?" *

A friend of the family, a doula, has been visiting me. She rubs my aching body in peppermint and lavender oils and the smell of them lingers in the apartment. She has filled a green ceramic pitcher with a tea of raspberry leaf, chamomile, fennel and peppermint. It's the first thing that has consistently worked to fight back the dull roar of nausea.

Sometime this week I awoke for the first time in five months without a headache. My belly is noticeably rounder, my face softer. Last night the baby gave the doula a solid kick well above my navel. It was the first time someone else could feel it. I cried.

I find myself again in the mystery of awe and joy and sadness. The pain that led me to Mary made me a better mother. I can't say whether it was worth the price I paid, but have learned to be grateful it wasn't my choice to make.

This pain, too, is not of my choosing. I wish I were the kind of woman who blossomed in pregnancy. I'm not. I glow, but it's from vomiting so hard.

I'm not even to the labor thing and already it's not as pretty as Jennifer Aniston in pigtails.

 Much of motherhood is jury-rigged – a thrown together contraption of dreams and wishes and the life that emerges quite without your input; held together with a little innate knowledge, tidbits from books and friends, and the help of people who sometimes just know better than you do – even about the things most sacred to you.

And sure, you can wear pigtails. But in labor, they kind of get in the way.

posted by Elizabeth at 10:12 p.m.

Yes, she took them home. She's gooood.

DUCKY
May 19, 2005

Cute Husband drove to New York to collect Mary and me. In the car on the way back, he told me Ducky had been in the hospital several days

Hyperemesis is two kinds of pain for me: the agony of brutal nausea and malnourishment; and the feeling of failure that I don't have the strength to do all the things that are important to me.

"You look much better, though," Cute Husband said. "You've had rest and now you can help her better."

He drove me to the hospital the next morning, where I found her, pale face framed by layers of gauze wrapped around her head. Her tiny body was draped in a hospital gown.

Auntie B hugged me hello before quickly heading home for a shower and a bite to eat. I took the seat beside my grandmother and tried to think of something mature, reassuring, comforting to say.

"Love the turban," was the best I could come up with.

"WHAT??" she shouted. "I'm afraid I can't hear you with this gauze over my ears. Horrid thing."

I smiled, and we looked awkwardly at each other for a minute before she pointed to the bottle of Ensure on the table in front of her.

"Quite good stuff, actually," she said. "I've been instructed to drink it."

I grinned and reached for the small cooler I had brought with me. "You have my sympathies," I said, pulling out one of the low-carb, high protein chocolate drink somethings Emily had found. They were yucky, but Cute Husband had insisted they were a prerequisite to spending the day at the hospital. He was out wandering around with Mare and I was pretty sure he was going to check the cooler to be sure I was keeping my promise.

"I'll drink if you will," I said, raising the small purple can toward her. We toasted and drank.

The summer I was pregnant with Mare I had lived with Ducky for part of the third trimester. I had never had greater sympathy for my grandmother: we both had strict diet requirements; couldn't lift much, or do as much as we wanted to; we tired easily and we peed a lot.

"Are you feeling better, then?" she asked conversationally. I wasn't about to get myself sent home, so I smiled and said, "Much." She nodded and said, "Me too," and we drank our drinks.

Two nurses came in to change the dressing on her head.

"I fell," Ducky said to me as gloved hands unwound the long strips of white.

"I know," I said. "I heard." I felt a dizzying rush of anger. Ducky had been admitted to the hospital for pneumonia. That first night they had left her unattended. She had woken, thinking she was at home, and gotten out of bed to go to the bathroom. She fell from the high hospital bed into a heap on the hard linoleum. The woman who had always stood so tall to me was bleeding on a hospital floor in the middle of the night and no one was helping her.

"It was in the emergency room," she clarified. I realized I was glaring at the woman changing her dressing; who had no responsibility for the fall whatsoever. I took a sip of the chocolate nasty.

After the woman was done cleaning the wound, I held the bandage in place and helped figure out the best way to get the gauze around her head. I smiled down at her and assured her the wound wasn't too bad. All I wanted to do was pull her into my arms and rock her to sleep. I settled for straightening her gown over her shoulder.

She smiled indulgently at me and I leaned in and said, "Would you like to know a secret?" I took out a pad of paper and scrawled three words and a little exclamation point.

"Are you sure?" she asked.

"The doctor was really sure," I grinned.

"Oh my." We laughed and passed a pleasant hour tossing out potential names and watching basketball on CNN highlights. ("That was a good shot," Ducky said of a rather impressive dunk by an athlete I couldn't begin to recognize and she probably couldn't see very well. "It sure was," I agreed.)

She ate her lunch when it came, and then fell asleep briefly. I listened to her breathe and read one of the mystery books on her night stand.

Auntie B returned, and we helped Ducky into a chair. She sat in the gown and the turban, her ankles carefully crossed.

The neurologist came in and briefed us on a recent CT scan.

"There's a little blood on the right side of her head," he said. "But nothing too serious."

"That's why she keeps waking up," I said. "She says her head hurts her on that side. ~ Is that the subdural hematoma they were talking about earlier?"

"Well," he laughed drolly, "it's hardly big enough to be called that."

This, too, was eerily like pregnancy: I looked at that smug young doctor and wondered if he'd ever loved a helpless person he had to entrust to a stranger.

He left and my aunt carefully reviewed with my grandmother what he had said and asked her if she had any questions. We helped her back to bed, and I gathered my things to go home.

"I'll be back after I feed the kids," my aunt said to her mother.

"And I'll be back in a few days," I added. She gestured me to come toward her.

"When you're my age," she said, nodding toward me and my aunt, "You'll be so glad you have *daughters*."

posted by Elizabeth at 12:20 a.m.

Hmm...Now We Know Why Toddlers Don't Vote

Sunday, May 22, 2005

Mare's two doll babies have recently been named "Cardamom" and "Tuna Sauce."

No. She will not be having any input into Baby Sister's name. 'Cause "Little Cardamom Tuna Sauce" deserves a future.

Today Mare is feeling:

posted by Elizabeth at 2:29 p.m.

DUCKY, PART II
Thursday, May 26, 2005

It was my greatest single test of womanly resolve: After a week of quiet panic that my grandmother would never be all right again she was finally awake and alert and sitting up looking at me. While eating pureed broccoli and tuna casserole.

And I still have killer morning sickness.

"I'm so glad you're feeling well enough to drive all this way to baby-sit me," she said when she settled into her chair for lunch. Slippery little thing.

"Oh, I'm sooooo much better," I said breezily.

"Because you in your condition are worth more to this family than I in mine."

"Well it's lucky I feel so great so we don't have to go thinking about such equations."

She raised her eyebrow. I raised mine, and we opened our lunches.

Mine was a turkey club wrap stuffed with veggies and mayo and bacon. It was sort of appealing, actually, until the nurse raised the lid off Ducky's plate, unleashing the smell of tuna and mashed broccoli. I stole just one glance at the two large puddles on her plate – one pea-green, the other paste-white – and swallowed.

Ducky wrinkled her nose delicately and said, "I have to eat to gain weight."

"Right," I said. "Me too. You clean your plate, and I'll... er... clean mine..." I raised the sandwich to my mouth and inhaled.

C'mon I've been a sport, I said to the God of Morning Sickness. I've barfed in snow, I've barfed in public trash cans, I've even barfed with the dog. I've been barfing for five long months. I just can't barf this time, that's all.

I took a cautious nibble of bacon and looked up at Ducky. She was old and small and grey. But she was still the same Ducky, her blue eyes looking out at the world in an impossibility of friendliness and indictment.

"Did I tell you about Mary and the hockey game in New York?" I asked. I had been wanting to tell her the story since it happened, how our sweet, tiny, tow-headed Mary had broken from the sidelines at her cousin Matthew's hockey game, how she picked up a stick and begged the coach to let her stay, how she got in there after the ball with a group of five year old boys. Ducky shook her head and laughed.

"You're in for a lot of work," she said.

"Yeah," I grinned, wondering what this other little girl was going to be like.

I didn't barf, and I did eat much of the sandwich.

I got back to El's house by late afternoon. Mare and Super-G had played together all day.

"Mare did great," Ellie reported. "She was tired and had a long nap and a diaper change... and I know someone who had corn for dinner last night."

"Oh. Sorry," I said.

"That's okay. I fed her All-Bran. Payback's a bitch."

It's nice to have friends.

On the way home from Miss Ellie's...

"Momma. I'm gonna have a baby sister."

"Yes you are."

"My sister's gonna be pink. Greta's gonna have a sister too, hers is gonna be brown."

"Poor Mr. Steve is going to be mightily confused."

Putting Greta to bed...

"Mommy?"

"Yes, Greta?"

"Maywee's gonna have a baby sister."

"Yes she is."

"Name's Tuna Sauce."

"Oh dear."

posted by Elizabeth at 11:23 a.m.

DAT BARBIE, DIS DWESS, AND STEP ON IT!
Wednesday, June 1, 2005

Mary has figured out my Achilles heel – I just don't do mornings. Rather than trying to ask me to feed her or some such nonsense, she just brings her toys into my bed and engages me in my weakened state.

"Momma? Hewp," she said this morning, poking a Barbie up my nose several times before I put my hands up to grasp it.

"On or off?" I muttered.

"Off," she chirped. With my eyes closed, I worked the tiny Velcro closures on a very pink ball gown, easing it down past Barbie's ergonomically impossible hips before I passed out again.

Seconds later, another Barbie crammed in my face.

"Dis Barbie wants dat dwess, dat Barbie wants dis dwess."

"Is this a want or a don't want?"

"Dis dwess goes on dat Barbie. Dat dwess goes on dis Barbie."

"Right, okay..." eyes closed, shimmying yet another ball gown off another buxom, rubbery female figure. I felt around, found the other dress, and worked it back up selfsame rubbery figure.

Back to sleep.

"Momma... Momma? Dis one next."

"'Kay. Right. Here I come." The dress was a nightmare of sparkly pink organza sleeves, and Barbie's pointy little hands kept getting stuck in the shoulder seam. I kept yanking until it tore and then just rammed the hand through and handed it back to the little blonde tyrant.

"Danks, Momma," she said.

"Momma's name is Momma," she told her Barbies, "and Ewizabef. Daddy's name is Daddy and Fwankwin. Baby Sister's name is Karenna. And Tuna Sauce." Another long pause, and then the familiar scent of plastic Barbie hair crammed toward my nostrils.

"On?" I muttered helplessly. "Off?"

"Dis Barbie wants dat dwess. Dat Barbie wants dis dwess."

"Oh, okay." Eyes closed, working the minuscule organza down Barbie's hips. The hole in the sleeve that had made things easy on the way down was making it hard on the way off – her little pointy thumb caught and I actually had to open my eyes to work it loose.

"Good job Momma! Now ~ dat dwess on dat Barbie, dis dwess on dis one."

"Right... okay... Here comes."

The same two Barbies passed the same two dresses between them three or four times this morning, assisted by a drooling, babbling woman who kept saying, "On? Off?"

Did I know? Did I realize I was being mercilessly suckered by a two foot chubbers ball of Barbie fascism? Or was I so asleep that each costume change seemed like a recurring nightmare?

Either way, Mary didn't care. What she knew was that at that hour I was a trained monkey, her trained monkey, and I switched those damned dresses at least three times before waking up enough to tell her no.

I just don't do mornings, folks.

posted by Elizabeth at 1:54 p.m.

Hewp! Barf!
Friday, June 3, 2005

Some people worry that they have too much crap in their lives.

I have too much barf.

This is what I was thinking as I used a bamboo skewer to prod regurgitated strawberries out of the tiny crevices of Mary's car seat. It was disassembled in my kitchen, the grey upholstery a pile of soggy vomitosis beside me. It had taken a screw driver, the instruction manual, and twenty minutes to get it off.

"I used to be a press secretary," I said to Miss Kate, through gags. "I wore darling suits. Ann Taylor. I could walk faster in a pair of pumps with a latte in hand than you can believe."

The strawberries were mixed with carrots, with a little lemonade thrown in for viscosity.

Mary and I had gone to lunch with my mother – a fancy girl's get together to celebrate my birthday. We missed the timing on the traffic and hit it just wrong – we were two hours bumper-to-bumper on the way back. Mary had barfed just twenty minutes from home, and it was spectacular.

I pulled over at a gas station and opened the door to a horror of vomit and devastated child.

"Mine dwess!" she sobbed, pointing to the pretty party dress she'd worn for the occasion.

"It's okay," I said, "Momma will fix it. You know Momma will fix it. It won't matter a bit."

I undid her car seat straps and she threw herself into my arms in a squishy hug. I fought gags and frustration: her dress was washable. Mine would now need a dry cleaner.

"Let's get your dress off, Bug," I said. Soon she was standing there in nothing but her best shoes and a diaper, her pretty hair style ruined, fresh tears running down her cheeks.

A car pulled up behind us, a man running into the gas station for a pack of cigarettes. Mare's face lighted up.

"Is he coming to help me?" she sniffled with big eyes.

A bolt of sick regret shuddered through me: I have always taught Mary that when someone is in pain, we stop to help. I have always told her to expect help and to ask for it.

She was naked, covered in vomit, and absolutely positive that someone was going to stop to help. I didn't know what to say. I had meant to instill perpetual optimism, but perhaps instead I have crippled her with unrealistic expectations of a world will never care as much about her as she thinks it should.

"Excuse me, can I help you out?"

I turned to see a grubby young teenager peering in at us. His boxers were showing at his waist, he was badly in need of a shave and some good facial cleanser – and he had just restored my faith in the world and my mothering.

"Oh, yes," I said. "Um... do you sell wipes?" I hoped he wouldn't notice the giant pack of them I had on the seat beside us.

"Yeah, hang on."

"He's helping!" Mary said.

"Of course he is," I said. "He saw you were sad and he came to see what he could do." The boy brought handi-wipes and I thanked him and gave her a few to swab around the vomitty car seat.

"Wheee!!" Mary said, climbing up on to the center console with a grin. "I'm NAKED!!"

Mare's despair had rallied me to action; her return to gleefulness was exhausting. Cute Husband was away on business, my car was a barf-bomb, the familiar rumbling in my belly told me lunch would not be staying down, and the road to bedtime seemed long and winding.

I have taught Mary to ask for help, and she has taught me to. I called Kate, our some-time babysitter, and she agreed to meet us at the house. She fixed Mare dinner while I barfed. She ran a bath and did the dishes while I hauled a bucket and some Lysol out to the car. I grabbed a bite while she coaxed Mary into a bath. The car seat cover was in the dryer by then, and all that was left was to reassemble the thing.

It's an Evenflo Triumph Five – this thing is massive, and it's got incredible safety ratings. The folks at Evenflo must really love kids – but they hate mommies.

The straps twist and wind and turn through all these loops and doohickeys. The instructions for disassembling show pictures of where everything comes out of, and that's fine, but at the end of the instructions it says, "To reassemble, follow directions in reverse."

Now anyone who has ever unfolded a road map knows that undoing something is a good deal simpler than doing it back up.

"I hate these people," I said to Miss Kate. It was ten o'clock and she and Mary were peering in at me as I resisted the urge to swear at the car seat. "It took me eight hours to get it back together last time," I said.

"How'd you do it?" Kate asked reasonably.

"Drank scotch. Eventually, it all made sense."

"Oh. Hmm."

"I have an idea, maybe you should drink scotch," I said, "Oh ... wait a minute. I think I have it! I think I... ah CRAPITTY CRAP CRAP CRAP!!!" I shouted.

"Momma, what's wong?" Mary said. "Oh, you sad?" She took my face in her hands. "Can I hewp you?" she asked with a tender pat on my back.

"You're a good helper, Boo," I said.

I finally sorta rammed the straps through in kinda the right places, and Kate offered to install it for me on her way out. I poured myself a pregnancy tea over ice in my cut crystal scotch glass.

Mary was tucked into her bed, a Barbie under each arm, her faith in humanity firmly in place. Perhaps the beauty of deciding to raise her to Believe is that I have to, too.

posted by Elizabeth at 9:28 p.m.

At Least I Remembered Underwear

Thursday, June 16, 2005

As I watched my daughter, little pigtails flying as she plunged toward Earth at sickening speed, my first thought was:

"Oh, shit I have no idea where the insurance card is."

You may be wondering what happened to me. So am I.

Late Tuesday night I got the word that the house we are living in has failed a state lead inspection.

Mary went to El's house Wednesday morning while I packed.

Two weeks ago Cute Husband began an internship in Albany. He has been living at my aunt and uncle's place in the Berkshires. When I told them what happened they eagerly upgraded the invitation from "Cute Husband for ten weeks" to "Cute Husband, kid, and pregnant lady indefinitely."

It's great to have family.

So I had some place to go. Kate came over to help me clear out, carefully hosing down the pink tricycle and Annabelle and her unfortunate friend Gippy the Baby with One Misdirected Eyeball. (There is no point in bugging out if you are taking the problem with you.) The good news is that I remembered most of the big ticket items, including underwear which I most often forget. The bad news is that somewhere in the chaos of the day, the cats ran away.

Ginny was thrilled to get in the car, though, because she didn't know I had made an appointment to drop her off at the kennel the next day in Lenox.

We left food on the porch for the cats.

It is officially Hotter than Blazes here in the Berkshires and I am increasingly pregnant and increasingly grumpy about it. I got dressed this morning and was now Displaced, Hotter than Blazes, Pregnant, Grumpy, and Really Hungry. I stepped outside to find Mary playing on the large swing set in the back yard, Cute Husband standing below, trying to coax her into the car.

"C'mon, Mare, Daddy's hungry," Cute Husband was saying.

"C'mon, hon," I added, "Momma's *homicidal.*"

"No. I LIKE it here!"

Here is where we did a bad, bad thing.

We turned and made for the car. Like we were leaving.

You know how people do that, right? Works every time. You fake the kid out, like you're going, but you're not really going, and like, everyone does that, right?

"NO MOMMA WAIT I WANNA COME WITH - AAAAAAAA!!!!"

Down she went, pigtails and all, hitting face first, spread eagled into the dirt.

This is where I thought about my insurance card. I haven't actually seen my wallet in about a month. The last time I saw it I was folding laundry and found it, kinda soggy, in the back pocket of my maternity shorts. I know right where I was standing, which pair of shorts it was, and what I had for breakfast that day. What I can't tell you is what I did with the damned thing afterward.

There is no fear in the world like "my-kid's-in-trouble" fear, and no guilt in this world like "She-just-wanted-to-be-with-me-bad-enough-to-fly" guilt.

There was no ice in the fridge, so when we found blood in Mary's mouth we fed her frozen corn. She loves corn.

"Don't leave without me!" she wept, clinging to me, spewing bloody frozen corn.

New rule in La Casa Looney Tunes: there's no more even *threatening* to leave without her.

It turned out that she was fine. She had the wind knocked out of her, and had bitten her tongue, and we've gotten to hear about that in great detail. She isn't too interested in the swing set any more, which is kind of a relief to me.

Over breakfast we made a plan: "You take Ginny to the kennel," Cute Husband said, "I'll make the drive home and get the cats." (He totally just wanted to climb back under the porch.)

When we got back to Emily's place, Ginny's collar and lead were lying in a very tidy pile on the porch - as though she had carefully removed them and put them neatly away before taking off.

"Okay, new plan," Cute Husband said. "You find the dog. I'm going to go hide in a corner and suck my thumb for a bit."

It was several hours of scouring the neighborhood, but we did find Ginny on a shady porch being fed treats by a nice old lady who commented that Ginny was far too fat. Ginny wolfed down the treats and looked fat and happy.

I got her over to the kennel with minutes to spare before closing time. It was ten o'clock before Cute Husband was able to round up the cats and come back.

Now here we are. Cute Husband is at work all day and I am alone with Mary. In the mountains. No friends. No posse. A swing set we're both monumentally afraid of. Nothing but Tuna Sauce and Gippy to keep us company.

Now if only I knew where my wallet was.

posted by Elizabeth at 11:46 p.m.

A Conversation with the Author

What made you start a blog?
I've heard people refer to writing as a craft, a calling, an art. It probably is all of those things. But to me, fundamentally, it is a discipline. My former boss, Keith Rupp, said a writer isn't someone who sits around waiting for inspiration and feeling profound. A writer is someone who consistently produces material on deadline regardless of how he or she feels about it.

It was very hard to be a writer after Mary was born. Sleep deprivation, toddler schedules and – yes, barf – slowly robbed me of the capacity to produce material on deadline.

So I discovered blogging. It wasn't prestigious and the deadlines were self-imposed – but it was published work I could churn out around play dates and mealtimes and naps. (Blogging? Grecian 5 Hair color for men? Not so different.)

Initially I had a few hundred hits per month, mostly from friends. But it started to catch on, I got better at it, and soon it was growing exponentially until I had tens of thousands of hits per month.

Why did you choose to self-publish a book?
The quick answer is because I was the only publisher I could find to publish me.

Who doesn't love that traditional success story of the agent, the bidding war for the manuscript, the hefty advance, the meteoric bestseller? But I'm not afraid to try it this way, first. The ability to publish books without regard for profit margins is the greatest revolution in media since the invention of the press. It changes everything. "Popular" is no longer synonymous with "successful" – and isn't that what we've all wanted since high school?

Do you have any tips for aspiring bloggers and writers?
I'll just pass along the answer that most helped me: write. Read. Practice. Don't be afraid to suck. I promise, you will suck. Don't skimp on the self-mockery.

As old Hebrew wisdom suggests, in one pocket carry a slip of paper that says, "You are the reason the Universe exists" in the other, a slip that says, "You are a speck of dirt."

You are both. Be both, write both.

If someone wants to contact you, what's the best way?
Drop me an e-mail at elizabeth@damomma.com I read every single one. I do answer them all personally; but it takes some time, so please be patient.

Coming Soon...

Volume II^{*, **, ***}

The pregnancy ends but the barfing goes on and on!

Learn about Mare's Zen meditation moments,
Elizabeth's breakdown at the Nissan dealership
and what everyone knows about Roo.

---

* *That's not the name of it. The truth is, I don't know what I'm going to call it. It took me three weeks, five drafts and a couple of gin and tonics to come up with "Motherhood is Not for Wimps" and that was already the name of my blog. So you see how hard it is. Hopefully the next title will be just as good and require a little less alcohol. Or just as good, at any rate.*

** *Of course, if no one buys this one, there won't be a second. So just FYI on that one. This is kind of an optimistic piece of advertising.*

*** *Of course, you're reading this, so maybe you bought it and you liked it so much you read all the way to the last page. You're a sport!*

Printed in the United States
111667LV00003B/290/A